What Do Our Children Know About Their Faith?

Results from the ACRE Assessment

John J. Convey, Ph.D.

National Catholic Educational Association

Second Printing 2010
ISBN No. 1-55833-438-6
Part No. ACR-24-1436

Contents

Foreword

This book contains an analysis of the results of a study of the ACRE assessment using data from the students in Catholic schools and those in parish religious education programs who took ACRE during the 2004-2005 school year. The analyses in the book follow the general pattern of the analyses using the 1994-1995 administration of ACRE that Andrew Thompson and I presented in our book, *Weaving Christ's Seamless Garment: Assessment of Catholic Religious Education*, which NCEA published in 1999.

In addition to providing an overview of the achievement of Catholic students on the faith knowledge section of ACRE, this study explores the personal beliefs and attitudes of Catholic students their faith, their sentiments about their personal religious practices, and their perceptions about their religion programs, their parishes and the seriousness of the problems they report being present in their schools. The study also identifies important predictors of the overall achievement of Catholic students in the knowledge of their faith, their agreement as to whether they attend Mass on weekends, and their feelings about their relationship with Jesus.

The book also presents recommendations on the use of ACRE to assist in the preparation of catechists, how ACRE could be improved when it is revised, and what research on ACRE and its data would be helpful in the future. An appendix in the book contains a collection of descriptions of best practices in religious education around the country as described by representatives from various dioceses, parishes and schools. The performance of their students on ACRE served as a basis for inviting the contributors to write about their program and how they use ACRE.

The book is intended for several audiences: national and diocesan religious education leaders, pastors, Catholic school principals and directors of parish religious education programs, catechists in schools and parish programs, book publishers, and parents as the primary educators of their children in the faith. It is hoped that each of these audiences will find information and suggestions in this book that will be helpful to them in improving the religious education of our Catholic children.

The contributions and encouragement of a number of people helped to make this book a reality. I extend my appreciation to all who assisted along the way, particularly:

Diana Dudoit Raiche, Director of the Department of Religious Education at NCEA, for her faith in my ability to write the book;

Christina Gergits, formerly Manager of NCEA Assessments, for her helpful comments on very early drafts of the manuscript;

Dr. John Poggio from the University of Kansas for providing the data for the analysis and for his helpful comments on the manuscript;

To those religious educators who contributed descriptions of their programs for the appendix:

Sister Jane Carew, OV, Director of Religious Education, Diocese of Fort Wayne-South Bend;

Brian Lemoi, Director of the Office of Evangelization and Lifelong Faith Formation, Diocese of St. Petersburg;

Sister Bernadette McManigal, BVM, Superintendent of Schools, Diocese of Arlington;

Sister Immaculate Paisant, MSC, Superintendent of Catholic Schools, Diocese of Houma-Thibodaux;

Alison J. Smith, Coordinator of Religious Education, St. Julie Billiart Parish, Hamilton, Ohio;

Karen Vogtner, Principal, St. John the Evangelist School, Hapeville, Georgia.

John J. Convey
St. Elizabeth Ann Seton Professor of Education
The Catholic University of America
December 2009

Preface

For over thirty years the National Catholic Educational Association has helped Catholic schools and parishes evaluate religion curriculum and programs with scientifically developed assessment tools. The Department of Religious Education assumed that responsibility after *Sharing the Light of Faith: National Catechetical Directory for Catholics of the United States* named NCEA as one of the collaborators expected to make such formal evaluation a reality.[1]

In response to this direction, NCEA began the process that Dr. John Convey describes in Chapter 1. The Department of Religious Education has remained faithful to shepherding the assessments, having revised the tool several times to keep pace with catechetical developments and documents as well as advancements in technology. These revisions have been collaborative efforts as originally envisioned.

The department has also been attentive to research based on the assessment data. This book is the third such research project concerning NCEA religious education assessments. It follows *That They May Know* by Andrew D. Thompson, Ph.D. and Fr. Paul Philibert, S.T.D., published in 1982 and *Weaving Christ's Seamless Garment: Assessment of Catholic Religious Education*, by John J. Convey, Ph.D. and Andrew D. Thompson, Ph.D., published in 1999.

In this volume, Dr. Convey addresses the outcomes of the 2001 revised ACRE, renamed Assessment for Catechesis/Religious Education to underscore the emphasis catechesis received in the *General Directory for Catechesis* (1997). He brings together a unique combination of history of the tool, experience as an educator, expertise as a researcher, and passion for Catholic education. I thank him for agreeing to address the religious education assessment data

---

[1] National Conference of Catholic Bishops. *Sharing the Light of Faith: National Catechetical Directory for Catholics of the United States* no. 222b. (Washington, DC: United States Catholic Conference, Department of Education, 1979), 137.

through the lens of *What Do Our Children Know About Their Faith?: Results from the ACRE Assessment*. His additional work in identifying sites with noteworthy outcomes made it possible to invite input from the field. This snap shot of how different locales use ACRE to their best advantage is sure to spark readers' imagination.

A project of this magnitude is the work of many gifted people. I echo Dr. Convey's thanks to the contributors of the "Best Practices" in Appendix B. Special thanks also goes to Christina Gergits, who worked in the religious education department from 2003-2009; Dr. John Poggio and Dr. Douglas Glasnapp, Co-Directors of the Center for Educational Testing and Evaluation at the University of Kansas and Dr. Joseph Pedulla of the Center for the Study of Testing Evaluation and Educational Policy at Boston College, the psychometric team that facilitated the 2001 revision; the NCEA production and marketing staff, Beatriz Ruiz and Wade Marshall; Elizabeth Ludvik, copy editor and our designer Deb Green.

It is our desire that this research will be a source of encouragement to schools and parishes as they strive to improve teaching, learning and formation in the Catholic faith. It may also suggest challenges and opportunities in response to the question: What do our Children Know About Their Faith?

Diana Dudoit Raiche
Executive Director
Department of Religious Education

Chapter 1
Introduction

What do Catholic students know about the Catholic faith? Do they know and understand the basic tenets of their religion? In what areas are they strong and where are they weak? And how well do they practice their faith? How effective is the religious instruction in our Catholic schools and parish programs? What are our children's opinions and sentiments about important aspects of the faith?

The Assessment of Catechesis/Religious Education (ACRE) from the National Catholic Educational Association (NCEA) provides a mechanism to help answer these and related questions. ACRE measures the knowledge of the faith and the beliefs, attitudes, practices and perceptions of elementary and secondary school students in Catholic schools and parish religious education programs. The assessment has three age-appropriate levels: Level 1 (ACRE1) for 5th graders, Level 2 (ACRE2) for 8th and 9th graders, and Level 3 (ACRE3) for 11th and 12th graders.

This book contains an analysis of ACRE using data from the students in Catholic schools and those in parish religious education programs who took ACRE during the 2004-2005 school year. The performance of Catholic students in Catholic schools and those in parish programs is compared overall and on an item-by-item basis to determine how well they know various aspects of their faith. In addition, the students' personal beliefs and attitudes toward their faith, their personal practices, and their perceptions about their religion programs, their parishes and problems in their schools are contrasted and compared. Finally, the most important predictors of overall achievement in Catholic students' knowledge of their faith, their attendance at Mass, and their feelings about their relationship with Jesus are identified.

Background

NCEA has assumed a leadership role in the assessment of the religious knowledge and attitudes of elementary and high school students in Catholic schools and parish religious education programs for over 30 years.

In 1975, NCEA established the first of two task forces of religious educators to develop instruments for the evaluation of religious education programs at the junior high and senior high school levels. The first task force with technical assistance from the Educational Testing Service consulted Church documents and leading Catholic theologians to produce the Religious Education Outcomes Inventory (REOI). REOI was first used in 1976 to measure the religious knowledge and attitudes of students in the 8th grade. REOI was revised in 1978 to simplify the language and stress a more personal approach to religious belief. The revised edition included two sections: (1) a 100-item religious knowledge inventory measuring the domains of God, Church, Sacraments, Christian Life, Scripture and Religious Terms and (2) a 40-item attitudinal survey.

A second task force developed the Religious Education Outcomes Inventory of Knowledge, Attitude and Practice (REKAP) in 1978 for use with high school students. REKAP included three sections: (1) a 60-item religious knowledge survey measuring the domains of Christian Doctrine, Christian Life, Sacred Scripture and Religious Terms; (2) a 30-item religious belief and attitude survey; and (3) a 20-item religious practice survey. In the book, *That They May Know You...*, Thompson (1982) provided a detailed description of REOI and REKAP along with an analysis of the performance between 1979 and 1981 of students in 8th grade on REOI and those in 11th and 12th grades on REKAP.

In 1989, NCEA combined REOI, REKAP, and an inventory developed for use with students in the middle elementary school grades, the Religious Education Inventory (REDI), into the Assessment of Catholic Religious Education (ACRE). In 1992, NCEA revised ACRE to include four sections: religious knowledge, personal beliefs and attitudes, personal practices, and perceptions about the students' schools, their parishes and themselves. The religious knowledge section contained seven items in each of seven domains (God, Church, Worship, Sacraments, Scripture, Morality, and Religious Terms) for ACRE1 and ACRE2 and an eighth domain (Christian Hope) for ACRE3. In their book, *Weaving Christ's Seamless Garment*, Convey and Thompson (1999) described the 1992 version of ACRE and provided an analysis of the performance of the students who took the assessment during the 1994-1995 school year.

In 2001, NCEA again revised ACRE and changed its name to the Assessment of Catechesis/Religious Education, while still retaining the acronym ACRE. The items for the 2001 edition of ACRE were based on domains using the *Protocol for Assessing the Conformity of Catechetical Materials with the Catechism of the Catholic Church, The General Directory for Catechesis*, and other Church documents on Catholic Social Teaching, as well as the 1992 version of ACRE. The revised edition contains two parts: Faith Knowledge (Part 1) and Beliefs, Attitudes, Practices and Perceptions (Part 2).

Reliability and Content Validity

Two important properties of an achievement measure of religious knowledge and a sentiment measure of beliefs, attitudes, practices and perceptions are the reliability and content validity of the measures. The reliability of an achievement test or a sentiment scale is a measure of the consistency or stability of the examinees' scores. Reliability is a necessary condition for a test or scale since an unreliable test or scale cannot be valid. The most relevant form of reliability for ACRE is its internal consistency, the extent to which the performance of examinees on similar items within ACRE is similar. Part I of ACRE has good reliability overall and within each of its domains and Part II has good reliability for each of its subscales. (See Appendix A for a description of the reliability of ACRE).

To help insure content validity, the items measuring faith knowledge on all three levels of ACRE came from a test blueprint that identified content domains based primarily on the *Protocol for Assessing the Conformity of Catechetical Materials with the Catechism of the Catholic Church*. A committee of theologians, educators and church leaders working from the blueprint for

3

the 1992 version of ACRE developed the test blueprint for the 2001 version. The expressed intent of the developers of ACRE was to create an "evaluative instrument that can be used by everyone regardless of the religion textbook series, provided that the series is in conformity with the Office for the Catechism at the United States Conference of Catholic Bishops" (*NCEA ACRE Interpretation Manual*, p. 2).

ACRE utilizes a domain-referenced assessment in which items are developed based on well-defined content domains. An assumption of such an assessment is that the items are randomly sampled from the particular domain. In practice, a random sampling of items doesn't occur. Rather, content experts write specific items that they judge are representative of each of the domains. While the assumption is that an infinite number of items are available for each domain, in practice only a limited number of items are developed. Thus, the results from each domain must be interpreted in the light of the particular items that actually are written. If a different set of items were developed from the domain, the performance of students might change accordingly, depending if the items were easier or more difficult or if they assessed more familiar or less familiar areas of the domain.

The test blueprint for ACRE was developed to assess specific objectives for faith knowledge in eight domains and to survey the beliefs, attitudes and practices in seven themes or subscales that were judged to be central to the faith of students at specific grades. The 2001 revision contains approximately one-third to one-half of the religious knowledge questions and about half of the sentiment items from the 1992 version of ACRE. The linkage for the religious knowledge items to the past edition is greatest for Level 1 and least for Level 3, whereas the linkage for the sentiment items is uniform across the three levels.

The importance of a test blueprint and adherence to it when writing items cannot be stressed too much. Matching items to a blueprint is the primary measure of the content validity of a test, which, for an achievement test of faith knowledge, is the most important type of validity of interest. The establishment of content validity is a judgmental process that, unlike reliability, is not dependent upon student performance, but rather on the expertise of the writers of the items and of the religious educators and testing professionals who reviewed them. Part I of ACRE, Faith Knowledge, appears to have good content validity. The evidence for the content validity of ACRE is presented in the Interpretation Manual for ACRE (*NCEA ACRE Interpretation Manual*, pp. 4-9).

Part 1: Faith Knowledge

The developers of the 2001 version of ACRE constructed items based on eight faith knowledge domains. Each domain has one or two objectives and a number of key concepts that assisted the item writers. The same domains are contained in each level of ACRE; however, the number, content and difficulty of the items are commensurate with the age and level of religious education of the students. The domains and key concepts that the developers and expert reviewers judged to be appropriate and more important at particular grade levels have more or fewer items associated with them.

A listing of the domains, their objectives and the number of items on each level of ACRE from the *NCEA ACRE Interpretation Manual* is presented in Table 1.1. The total number of items on ACRE1 is 51, on ACRE2, 57, and on ACRE3, 63. For a more complete description of the domains and the assessment structure, see the *NCEA ACRE Interpretation Manual.*

Table 1.1 Faith Knowledge Domains

Domain	Objective	Number of Items		
		ACRE1	ACRE2	ACRE3
1. God	Know and understand basic Catholic teaching about God as Father, Son, and Holy Spirit	6	7	8
2. Church	Understand the origin, mission, structure, community and membership of the Church	5	8	8

Table 1.1 Faith Knowledge Domains, continued

Domain	Objective	Number of Items		
		ACRE1	ACRE2	ACRE3
3. Liturgy	• Know about the Church's liturgical life in terms of liturgical feasts, seasons, symbols, religious practices and concepts of prayer. • Know and understand the sacraments as signs and instruments of grace.	9	8	7
4. Revelation, Scripture, Faith	• Recognize Scripture as God's inspired word. • Know the major divisions of the Bible, the chief persons in biblical history, and major biblical themes from the Old and New Testaments.	7	6	8
5. Life in Christ	• Know the teachings of Jesus and the Church as the basis of Christian morality and understand Catholic Social Teaching. • Be aware of the importance of a well-formed conscience for decision-making.	7	10	10
6. Church History	Become familiar with the central stories, key events and major figures that have shaped the history and development of the Church overtime as appropriate for the student's grade level.	4	6	8
7. Prayer / Religious Practice	Recognize and learn how to engage in Catholic forms of personal prayer and ways of deepening one's spiritual life.	6	5	8
8. Catholic Faith Literacy	Be literate in the use of Catholic religious terminology.	7	7	6
	Total Number of Items	51	57	63

Pillars of the Catechism

Since the items for ACRE were developed in accord with the *Protocol for Assessing the Conformity of Catechetical Materials with the Catechism of the*

Catholic Church, in addition to reporting by domains, the results of ACRE are also reported to the schools and parishes according to the four parts or pillars of the Catechism. The structure of the *Catechism of the Catholic Church* follows the same order as the catechism of St. Pius V, with the material arranged in four parts: Creed, Liturgy and Sacraments, Christian Way of Life, and Christian Prayer (Pope John Paul II, *Fidei Depositum,* in the *Catechism of the Catholic Church,* United States Catholic Conference, p. 4). Table 1.2 shows the number of items at each level of ACRE for each of the pillars of the Catechism.

Table 1.2 Number of ACRE Items on each Pillar of the Catechism

Pillar	ACRE1	ACRE2	ACRE3
1. Profession of Faith (The Creed)	12	14	16
2. Celebration of the Christian Mystery (Liturgy and Sacraments)	12	14	13
3. Life in Christ (Morality)	12	13	15
4. Christian Prayer (Prayer)	10	11	11

Part 2: Personal Beliefs, Attitudes, Practices and Perceptions

Part 2 of ACRE measures the personal beliefs, attitudes, practices and perceptions of the students. Most of the items in Part 2 of the 2001 version of ACRE were also contained in the 1992 version. In some cases, however, the scale response changed from a frequency continuum (Always-Never) to an agreement continuum (Strongly Agree – Strongly Disagree) and the number of scale steps changed from 3 steps (Always, Sometime, Never) to 4 steps (Strongly Agree, Agree, Disagree, Strongly Disagree). The change from a frequency scale to an agreement continuum results in a different interpretation of the results, particularly on items that describe behavior like attending Mass. The 1992 version, albeit self-reported by a student, permitted an interpretation of how frequently a student attended Mass. On the other hand, on the 2001 version, if a student strongly agreed that he or she attended Mass on weekends, does that translate to attending every weekend? And what if a student responded that they disagreed to that statement, what can be said about the frequency of his or her attendance? Because of the differences in scale and number of scale steps from 3 to 4, the findings of the 2001 version of Part 2 are not directly comparable to the results of the 1992 version.

Subscale Definitions

Part 2 contains seven subscales: Relationship with Jesus, Image of God, Catholic Identity, Morality, Family Relationships/Communication, Religion Program/Parish, and Vocation. Level 1 contains 27 items, Level 2 contains 33 items and Level 3 contains 34 items. Table 1.3 contains a listing of the items that correspond to these various subscales.

Table 1.3 Items for Subscales in Part 2

Subscale	Items	ACRE		
		I	II	III
Relationship with Jesus	Jesus' relationship with me really helps me	x	x	x
	I believe that Jesus cured the blind and raised the dead	x	x	x
	I feel Jesus really understands me	x	x	x
	I look upon Jesus as my Savior and friend	x	x	x
Image of God	I think of God as a strict judge (reverse scored)	x	x	x
	My friends and I talk about God [1]	x	x	x
	One way that God speaks to me is through the Bible [2]	x	x	x
	When I pray, God really does listen to me	x	x	x
	Even when I sin, God still loves me	x	x	x
	I would like to learn how to get closer to God			x
Catholic Identity [3]	I attend Saturday evening/Sunday Mass	x	x	x
	Praying the rosary is important to me	x	x	x
	I participate in the sacrament of Penance	x	x	x
	Being a Catholic is important to me	x	x	x

---

[1] This item was originally on the Relationship with Others subscale, but was moved to the Images of God subscale based on the results of a factor analysis performed by the author.

[2] This item was originally on the Relationship with Jesus subscale, but was moved to the Images of God subscale on the basis of the results of factor analysis performed by the author.

Table 1.3 Items for Subscales in Part 2, continued

Subscale	Items	ACRE		
		I	II	III
Morality	It is all right to try drugs (reverse scored)	x	x	x
	It is OK to copy a friend's homework if you do not have time to get yours done (reverse scored)	x	x	x
	My friends and I talk about moral issues			x
	My friends and I talk about things that are right or wrong	x	x	
	I take time to think about whether my actions are right or wrong	x	x	x
	It is OK for people my age to drink alcohol at a party (reversed)		x	x
	It is all right for a couple to live together before getting married (reversed)		x	x
	It is important to me to wait until marriage before having sexual intercourse		x	x
	I think abortion is wrong under any condition		x	x
	I am personally responsible for making the world a better place		x	x
Family Relationships / Communication[4]	If I thought a friend were getting addicted to drugs or alcohol, I would talk to an adult I trust		x	x
	Gathering together for the family meal, whenever possible, is important to my family	x	x	x
	I talk about most serious issues with one or both of my parents	x	x	x
	My family prays together at home	x	x	x

---

[3] The item about vocations that was originally on the Catholic Identity subscale was moved to a single item scale based on the results of factor analysis performed by the author.

[4] In the NCEA ACRE *Interpretation Manual,* this subscale was named "Relationships with Others" and contained 5 items instead of 4 items.

Table 1.3 Items for Subscales in Part 2, continued

Subscale	Items	ACRE		
		I	II	III
Religion Program / Parish	I am glad to be in this school/parish religion program	x	x	x
	Some of my religion teachers have been a positive influence on how I think and live	x	x	x
	Our religion program encourages us to do volunteer work	x	x	x
	Students here really care about each other	x	x	x
	I belong to an excellent parish	x	x	x
	People in my parish care about helping others	x	x	x
Vocation	I have thought about becoming a sister, priest or brother	x	x	x
	Total Number of Items	27	33	34

Table 1.4 Perceived Problems at School

Problem	ACRE1	ACRE2	ACRE3
Teasing, bullying, name-calling	x	x	
Cursing, blasphemy, swearing	x	x	x
Cheating, lack of honesty	x	x	x
Fighting	x	x	x
Respect for diversity	x	x	x
Personal safety	x	x	x
Drugs	x	x	x
Alcohol	x	x	x
Racism	x	x	x
Sexual harassment		x	x
Date rape		x	x
Eating disorders		x	x
Marijuana		x	x

Perceptions of Problems

In addition to the domains assessing various beliefs, attitudes, practices and perceptions, Part 2 of ACRE assessed the extent to which students felt that various issues were problems in their schools. The students were asked to indicate whether each issue was a big problem, a minor problem or not a problem at their individual schools. Table 1.4 shows the problems that the students at each level of ACRE were asked to address.

Summary

In summary, ACRE Part 1 and ACRE Part 2 are well constructed measures that are reliable with good content validity. As such, the results from ACRE are useful to dioceses and schools as measures of students' religious knowledge and a gauge of their beliefs, attitudes, practices and perceptions. The measures, however, are not perfect and could be improved. The subsequent chapters will present evidence about the strengths and limitations of each of the measures and suggestions as to how to improve them. In addition, evidence will be presented as to how well students in Catholic schools and those in parish programs perform on ACRE and point to areas of strengths and weakness in these students' religious knowledge, beliefs, attitudes, practices and perceptions.

Overview of Subsequent Chapters

Chapter 2 contains a description of the data and the results of the analyses of the overall achievement of students on Part 1 and Part 2. The chapter presents the average achievement in faith knowledge of the students in Catholic schools, both Catholic and non-Catholic, and students in parish religious education programs. Next, the performance of Catholic students is examined for the eight domains of Part 1, Faith Knowledge, and the seven subscales of Part 2, Beliefs, Attitudes, Practices and Perceptions.

Chapter 3 presents a detailed analysis of the performance of Catholic students on the items in the first four domains of Faith Knowledge: God, Church, Liturgy and Sacraments, and Revelation, Scripture and Faith.

Chapter 4 presents a detailed analysis of the performance of Catholic students on the items in the remaining four domains of Faith Knowledge: Life in Christ, Church History, Prayer and Religious Practice, and Catholic Faith Literacy.

Chapter 5 presents the performance of students on the items that comprised the seven subscales: Relationship with Jesus, Images of God, Catholic Identity, Moral Judgments, Family Relationships/Communication, Perceptions of the Religion Program/Parish, and Vocations. In addition, the chapter contains a summary of the perceptions of students about the relative seriousness of various problems that occur in their schools.

Chapter 6 contains the results of analyses used to identify the important predictors of students' achievement in faith knowledge, their reported attendance at Mass, and the degree of their reported relationship with Jesus.

Chapter 7 presents a summary of the findings of the results of the analyses of Faith Knowledge and of Beliefs, Attitudes, Practices and Perceptions across the three levels of ACRE. The overall performance of the students on the specific themes is also discussed. Finally, the chapter contains recommendations concerning the preparation of catechists, more emphasis on an intentional catechesis, how ACRE could be improved when it is revised, and future research on ACRE and its data.

Appendix A contains a description of the reliability of ACRE Part 1 and ACRE Part 2.

Appendix B contains a collection of best practices in religious education around the country as described by representatives from various dioceses, parishes and schools. The performance of their students on ACRE served as a basis for inviting the contributors to write about their program and how they use ACRE.

Chapter 2
Data and General Findings

This chapter presents a summary of the performance on the ACRE assessment for the students from the 2004-2005 year. The first section of the chapter contains a description of the data and their limitations. The analysis of the differences between the students in Catholic schools, both Catholics and non-Catholics, and students in parish religious education programs is then presented. Following the reporting of the mean differences and percent correct for the total scores on faith knowledge, comparisons are reported relative to the pillars of the Catechism and the attainment of proficiency levels that have been established by NCEA. The next section presents the summary findings regarding the eight domains of Part 1, Faith Knowledge. The final section contains the summary for Part 2 of ACRE regarding beliefs, attitudes, practices and perceptions. The analysis of students' perceptions of problems in their schools is presented in Chapter 5.

Some tables in this chapter and in subsequent chapters contain a statistic called the "effect size." This statistic describes the relative magnitude in standard deviation units of the differences between the means of the students in Catholic schools and those in parish programs[1]. Non-Catholic students in Catholic schools are not included in these comparisons. The effect size is used in lieu of statistical tests of the significance of differences between the means, since the number of students in each analysis is so large that extremely small differences are statistically significant; however, such small difference while statistically significant are not meaningful in practice. The effect size does not depend on the sample size and is thus a better indicator of the relative sizes of the differences than the statistical tests would be. In keeping with commonly

---

[1] The effect size is defined as the absolute value of the difference between two means divided by the standard deviation, i.e., $|M1 - M2|/SD$

accepted statistical norms for describing the size of effects and for the procedure used to determine effects size in this book, effect sizes less than .25 are
considered to be small, those between .25 and .75 to be medium, and those
greater than .75 to be large (Cohen, 1988).

The Data

The data for the analyses in the study are from students in Catholic schools
and parish-based religious education programs who took ACRE during the
2004-2005 school year. The 2004-2005 administration was selected since it
represented 10 years since the analysis of ACRE using the 1994-1995 data
(Convey & Thompson, 1999). The use of one year of data provides a reason-
able but limited basis for the analysis. The use of data over multiple years
would provide a more comprehensive, although not necessarily different,
pattern of responses to items on Part 1 and Part 2.

Table 2.1 shows the distribution of the examinees in 2004-2005 by level
of ACRE and type of program. The total number of examinees in the analysis
included in the analysis is 163,347 from 115 dioceses for ACRE1, 101 dioceses
for ACRE2 and 79 dioceses for ACRE3. Data from approximately 9,000
additional students who took ACRE during 2004-2005 were not used in the
study because of various coding issues. Seventy-seven percent of the examinees
in the dataset are Catholic students attending Catholic schools, 12 percent are
from parish religious education programs and 11 percent are non-Catholic
students attending Catholic schools. Over 300 parish programs are represented
on ACRE1 and ACRE2 and just fewer than 100 on ACRE3.

Table 2.1 Number of Examinees in 2004-2005
by Group and Level of ACRE

Level	Catholics in Catholic School	Non-Catholics in Catholic Schools	Parish Programs	Total
ACRE1	47,504	5,256	9,567	62,327
ACRE2	55,006	7,702	8,575	71,283
ACRE3	23,225	5,405	1,107	29,737
Total	125,735	18,363	19,249	163,347

Limitations of the Data

The students in the analysis are not a random sample of students in Catholic schools and parish religious education programs across the United States and neither can they be since dioceses, schools and parishes choose to take ACRE and are not selected at random beforehand. In addition, it is possible that the results are not representative of the entire nation, since only about half of the dioceses in the United States are represented in the ACRE1 and ACRE2 datasets and only about a third of dioceses in the ACRE3 dataset. Furthermore, not every school and parish in the dioceses that are represented participated in the assessment. Therefore, since the sample is not scientific, the results may not apply to all Catholic students in all Catholic schools and parish religious education programs. There is no way of knowing to what extent the sample is representative of the population of all students. Therefore, without obtaining additional information and performing additional analyses, any interpretation about the extent of the knowledge of the faith on the part of Catholic students, their beliefs and attitudes, and differences between Catholics students in Catholic schools and those in parish religious education programs must be made with caution.

Another limitation of the data is that students don't all take ACRE at the same time during the school year. For example, approximately 10 percent of the students took ACRE1 exam prior to January, almost 50 percent took it in January and February, and the remaining 40 percent took it later in the year. Thus, those who took the test later in the year had the advantage of more religious instruction, particularly those in Catholic schools, where religion is taught every day or several times a week, and this may have influenced their performance on Part 1 of ACRE, the assessment of their knowledge of the faith. Taking ACRE at different times of the year should not have any measurable impact, however, on the performance of students on Part 2 since the sentiments measured there are fairly stable and not necessarily directly influenced by instruction as would be the case with religious knowledge.

An additional limitation is the cross-sectional nature of the data. The students who took the different levels of ACRE are not the same. As a result it is not possible to make longitudinal interpretations regarding how students have grown in their understanding of the faith from the 5th grade to the 8th grade and into high school.

ACRE Part 1: Knowledge of the Faith

Group Comparisons

Table 2.2 shows the average total scores on the three levels of Part 1 of ACRE for Catholic students in Catholic schools, non-Catholic students in Catholic schools and Catholic students in parish religious education programs. The only trend evident in the comparisons of the scores across the three levels of ACRE is that, for each level of ACRE, Catholic students in Catholic schools have the highest scores, followed by non-Catholic students in Catholic schools, and finally by Catholic students in parish religious education programs. Using the designations about the size of the effects described earlier, the differences between the average scores of Catholic students in Catholic schools and those in parish programs are large on ACRE1 (effect size = .81) and ACRE2 (effect size = .88) and medium on ACRE3 (effect size = .44).

Catholic students in Catholic schools had the best performances of all groups on the Faith Knowledge sections of ACRE1 and ACRE2, answering approximately three-quarters of the items correctly on each level. Compared with Catholic students in Catholic schools, non-Catholic students in Catholic schools answered, on average, four fewer items correctly on ACRE1 and ACRE2 and students in parish programs answered correctly, on average, six fewer items on ACRE1 and eight fewer items on ACRE2.

The differences between the three groups of students were smaller on ACRE3. Catholic students in Catholic schools still answered more items correctly, about 71 percent. Both non-Catholics in Catholic schools and students in parish religious education programs correctly answered about five fewer questions than did the Catholic students who attended Catholic schools.

Table 2.2 Average Scores on ACRE Part 1
by Level and Group of Students

	Catholics in Catholic School	Non-Catholics in Catholic Schools	Catholics in Parish Programs	Total	Effect Size [2]
ACRE1 (51 items)					
Percent Correct	74.8%	67.1%	62.7%	72.3%	
Mean[3]	38.15%	34.20	31.98	36.87	.81
SD [4]	7.17%	7.98	7.59	7.67	
ACRE2 (57 items)					
Percent Correct	75.3%	66.4%	60.6%	72.5%	
Mean	42.90	37.84	34.52	41.35	.88
SD	8.72	10.18	9.58	9.47	
ACRE3 (63 items)					
Percent Correct	71.0%	63.7%	62.9%	69.4%	
Mean	44.75	40.12	39.64	43.72	.46
SD	10.92	12.26	10.98	11.35	

Pillars of the Catechism

Table 2.3 shows the performance of the students at each level of ACRE on the items that correspond to each of the pillars of the Catechism. Recall that the pillars were formed by reclassifying the items from the eight domains. The students who took ACRE1 (79% correct) and ACRE3 (76% correct) did best

---

[2] The effect size is the difference between the means of Catholics in Catholic schools and Catholics in parish programs divided by the overall standard deviation. A positive effect size indicates that the students in Catholic schools had higher mean scores on the domain than the students from parish religious education programs. A negative effect size indicates that the parish religious education students had higher means than the students from Catholic schools.

[3] The mean represents the average score, the number of correct answers.

[4] SD represents the standard deviation, which is a measure of the amount of variability in the scores. On all three levels of ACRE, the scores of Catholic students in Catholic schools had the least amount of variability and the scores of non-Catholic students had the most variability.

on the items on those tests that related to the Creed, while the students who took ACRE2 did best on the items that related to Prayer (79% correct) and Morality (77% correct). On all levels, however, the performance across the pillars was fairly homogeneous with the differences in the percentage of correct answers from the pillar with the highest scores to the pillar with the lowest scores being less than 10 percent.

As was the case in the overall mean scores (Table 2.2), Catholic students in Catholic schools performed best on the pillars. Except for the items on Morality in ACRE3 (67% correct), Catholic students in Catholic schools scored 70 percent or higher on the pillars across the three levels. On the other hand, Catholic students in parish programs scored higher than 70 percent only on the Creed in ACRE1 and they scored 60 percent or lower on the remaining pillars on ACRE1 and on the Creed (56%) and Liturgy and Sacraments (56%) on ACRE2.

Table 2.3 Average Percent Correct on the Pillars of the Catechism

	Catholics in Catholic School	Non-Catholics in Catholic Schools	Catholics in Parish Programs	Total
ACRE1				
Creed	82%	76%	71%	79%
Liturgy and Sacraments	73%	65%	60%	70%
Morality	70%	64%	60%	68%
Prayer	73%	65%	58%	70%
ACRE2				
Creed	73%	64%	56%	70%
Liturgy and Sacraments	72%	61%	56%	69%
Morality	79%	71%	67%	77%
Prayer	82%	74%	68%	79%
ACRE3				
Creed	77%	70%	69%	76%
Liturgy and Sacraments	72%	62%	64%	70%
Morality	67%	62%	62%	66%
Prayer	70%	63%	63%	69%

Proficiency Levels

With the 2001 revision of ACRE, NCEA (*NCEA ACRE Interpretation Manual*, p. 21) established three levels of performance: Advanced, Proficient and Needs Improvement. The following definitions were used:

- Students performing at the Advanced level, defined as correctly answering at least 86 percent of the items (88% on ACRE1), consistently demonstrate "superior knowledge and understanding of the faith knowledge assessed appropriate to the student's age and stage of faith formation."

- Students performing at the Proficient level, defined as correctly answering 64 percent to 86 percent of the items correctly, demonstrate "satisfactory knowledge and understanding of the faith knowledge assessed with evidence of acceptable command of key concepts that support core faith themes and domains assessed appropriate to age and stage of formation."

- Students performing at the Needs Improvement level, defined as correctly answering less than 64 percent of the items, demonstrate a "below-basic knowledge and understanding of the faith knowledge assessed that is not yet fully satisfactory for the age and stage of faith formation."

Table 2.4 shows the percentage of Catholic students in Catholic schools and parish programs performing at each of the proficiency levels. Across the three levels of ACRE, similar patterns emerge.

- Between 20 and 30 percent of Catholic students in Catholic schools scored at the Advanced level and between 50 and 60 percent scored at the Proficient level. Thus, across the three levels of ACRE, 80 percent of Catholic students in Catholic schools on ACRE1, 79 percent on ACRE2, and 70 percent on ACRE3 met the expectations of catechetical leaders.

- On the other hand, 16 to 21 percent of Catholic students in parish programs scored at the Advanced level and 39 to 43 percent scored at the Proficient level. Therefore, 48 percent of students in parish programs on ACRE1, 44 percent on ACRE2 and 50 percent on ACRE3 met the expectations of catechetical leaders.

- Overall, a significant number of students, between 20 and 30 percent of Catholic students in Catholic schools and more than half (50% to 56%) of Catholic students in parish programs, had scores that fell into the Needs Improvement category.

Table 2.4 Distribution of Proficiency Scores of Catholic Students

	Catholics in Catholic School	Catholics in Parish Programs	Total
ACRE1			
Advanced	20%	5%	16%
Proficient	60%	43%	57%
Needs Improvement	20%	52%	27%
ACRE2			
Advanced	25%	5%	21%
Proficient	54%	39%	52%
Needs Improvement	21%	56%	27%
ACRE3			
Advanced	20%	9%	18%
Proficient	50%	41%	49%
Needs Improvement	30%	50%	33%

Parish Programs: 8th Grade - 9th Grade Differences

The enrollment of Catholic students in parish programs beyond the 8th grade typically declines from the numbers enrolled up to 8th grade. The students who continue with their formal religious education in parish programs typically are those who are more highly motivated and/or who have strong family support and expectations for their religious education. It might be expected that the performance of these students would exceed the performance of those who end their formal religious education in 8th grade.

Table 2.5 provides some evidence of the higher performance of those students who continue their religious education in parish programs past the elementary grades. The table shows the average performance on ACRE2 for those students in 8th grade or lower compared with the relatively small number (n = 598) of students already in high school who continue in parish programs. The percent correct and means of those already in high school (typically in the 9th grade program of a parish, although it may be that some of these students also attended a Catholic high school as well) exceed the corresponding scores for the students who are still in elementary school.

Table 2.5 Scores on ACRE2 for Students in Parish Programs

ACRE2	8th Grade and Lower	9th Grade and Higher
Percent Correct	60.3%	65.1%
Mean	34.36	37.12
SD	9.55	9.55
n	7,924	598
Pillars of the Catechism		
Creed	56%	61%
Liturgy and Sacraments	56%	60%
Morality	67%	73%
Prayer	67%	72%

Faith Knowledge Domain Scores

Figures 2.1 to 2.3 show the distribution of the average percentage of correct answers on each domain achieved by Catholic students in Catholic schools and those in parish religious education programs for each level of ACRE. The domains in the graphs are arranged in descending order from the domain with the highest percentage of correct answers to the domain with the lowest percentage of correct answers. The graphical displays provide a visual representation of the findings in Table 2.2, that is, Catholic students in Catholic schools score better in each domain than Catholic students in parish religious education programs.

Chapter 3 and Chapter 4 contain a more complete analysis of the performance of the students on the Faith Knowledge domains and their individual items.

ACRE1

On ACRE1 (Figure 2.1) students scored highest on the domain of God-Father, Son, and Holy Spirit and lowest on domain of Church History. Catholic students in Catholic schools scored above 80 percent correct on the God domain and the Revelation, Scripture and Faith domain; between 70 percent and 80 percent on Catholic Faith Literacy, the Church domain, and Liturgy and Sacraments; and between 60 percent and 70 percent on Prayer/Religious Practices, Life in Christ (Morality/ Catholic Social Teaching) and Church History. The performance of the students from parish religious education programs on the comparable domains is on average approximately 10 percentage points lower than that of Catholic students in Catholic schools.

Figure 2.1 Average Percent Correct by Group – ACRE1

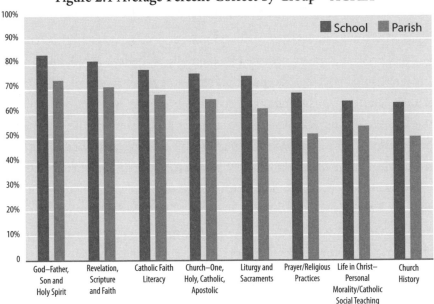

ACRE2

On ACRE2 (Figure 2.2) students scored highest on the God domain and lowest on the Church History domain, similar to how the students in ACRE1 scored. While some differences occurred in the relative percentages of correct answers and the relative order of the domains, the pattern of scores on ACRE2 was quite similar to ACRE1, except the differences between those in Catholic schools and those in parish program were greater on ACRE2 than they were on ACRE1. Students in Catholic schools scored above 80 percent correct on the God domain, between 60 percent and 70 percent on the domains of Catholic Faith Literacy and Church History, and between 70 percent and 80 percent on the remaining five domains. On the other hand, students from parish programs scored between 60 percent and 70 percent on four domains, between 50 percent and 60 percent on three other domains, and less than 50 percent on the Church History domain.

Figure 2.2 Average Percent Correct by Group – ACRE2

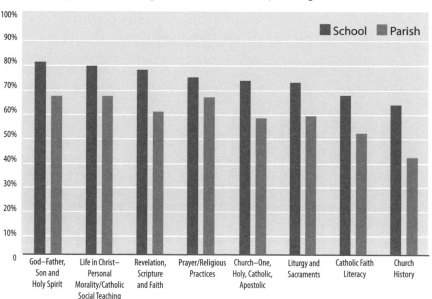

ACRE3

On ACRE3 (Figure 2.3) a different pattern emerges than the patterns observed in ACRE1 and ACRE2. While still present, the difference in the average scores of students in Catholic schools and parish programs diminishes. Those in Catholic schools continue to score higher than those in parish programs on each domain; however, the difference exceeds 10 percentages points on only two domains: Catholic Faith Literacy and Revelation, Scripture and Faith.

As was alluded to in the discussion of Table 2.5, students who continue in parish religious education programs through their high school years are likely to be active Catholics with strong family support. As analyses in Chapter 6 will demonstrate and other studies have found (Convey & Thompson, 1999; Convey, 1992), such family support is highly predictive of stronger religious practice and higher levels of faith knowledge. As a result, it is not surprising that the differences in faith knowledge of students in Catholic schools and those in parish religious education programs are smaller for students who took ACRE3 than they were for students who took ACRE1 or ACRE2.

Figure 2.3 Average Percent Correct by Group – ACRE3

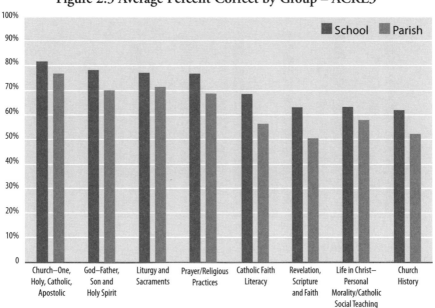

ACRE Part 2: Beliefs, Attitudes, Practices and Perceptions

Table 2.6 shows the average scores for Catholic students in Catholic schools and those in parish religious education programs for each of the subscales of Part 2. The highest ratings from the students are for their relationship with Jesus and for their sentiments towards their parishes.

The difference in sentiments between Catholic students from Catholic schools and those from parish program across the three levels of ACRE is generally small. Of the 21 comparisons in Table 2.6, 15 of the effect sizes are small (less than .25) and six are in the medium range (between .25 and .75). There are no large differences in the sentiments of Catholic students from Catholic schools and those from parish programs.

The greatest differences between the two groups of students occur on the Catholic Identity subscale of ACRE1 in favor of Catholics in Catholic schools (effect size = .70) and on four subscale on ACRE3, all in favor of students in parish programs: Catholic Identity (effect size = -.43), Parish (effect size = -.36), Morality (effect size = -.40), and Relationship with Jesus (effect size = -.29).

The sentiments of both groups across the subscales are more homogeneous on ACRE2 than on ACRE1 and ACRE3. Contrary to the patterns observed in Part 1 regarding achievement in faith knowledge, students in parish programs occasionally had more favorable sentiments toward the various issues raised than did students from Catholic schools. For example, students from parish programs had higher scores than students in Catholic schools on all the subscales of ACRE3 and two of the subscales (Morality and Parish) of ACRE1 and ACRE2.

Table 2.6 Average[5] Subscale Scores for ACRE Part 2

Subscale [6]	Catholics in Catholic Schools	Catholics in Parish Programs	Effect Size [7]
ACRE1			
Relationship with Jesus	3.67	3.58	.21
Image of God	3.32	3.25	.18
Catholic Identity	3.61	3.24	.70
Morality	3.34	3.36	−.05
Family Relationships/Communication	3.19	3.18	.02
Religion Program	3.18	3.13	.10
Parish	3.60	3.62	−.04
ACRE2			
Relationship with Jesus	3.48	3.43	.09
Image of God	3.13	3.11	.04
Catholic Identity	3.12	3.07	.08
Morality	3.03	3.07	−.09
Family Relationships/Communication	2.97	2.96	.02
Religion Program	2.98	2.89	.18
Parish	3.35	3.36	−.02
ACRE3			
Relationship with Jesus	3.24	3.44	−.29
Image of God	3.00	3.13	−.26
Catholic Identity	2.79	3.11	−.43
Morality	2.77	2.98	−.40
Family Relationships/Communication	2.81	2.91	−.17
Religion Program	3.01	3.02	−.02
Parish	3.07	3.35	−.36

[5] The scale scores (4=Strongly Agree, 3=Agree, 2=Disagree, 1=Strongly Disagree) are averaged. The scale values for items that are negatively stated are reversed prior to calculating the average score.

[6] The Religion Program/Parish subscale is divided for purposes of this analysis to illustrate the differences in the mean scores for the religion program and the parish.

[7] As in previous tables, positive values for the effect size indicate that Catholic schools had higher scores than parish programs and negative values indicate that the parish programs had the higher scores.

Figure 2.4 and Figure 2.5 show the average sentiments across the three levels of ACRE for Catholic students in Catholic schools and for students in parish religious education programs, respectively. In general, for each subscale the average sentiment score declines from the youngest cohort of students (ACRE1) to the oldest cohort (ACRE3). This pattern of decline is more evident for students in Catholic schools than for students from parish programs. For Catholic students in Catholic schools the decline in sentiment is most noticeable for the subscales of Relationship with Jesus, Catholic Identity, Perceptions of Parish and Moral Judgments. The most notable decline in the sentiments of students in parish religious education programs is for the subscale of Moral Judgments. Chapter 5 presents a more detailed analysis of the subscales in Part 2 and their individual items.

Figure 2.4 Average Scores of Catholic Students in Catholic Schools

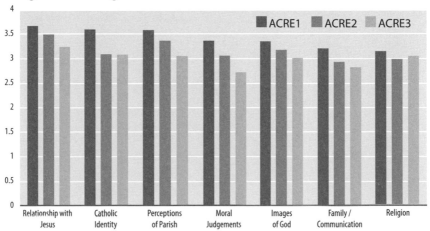

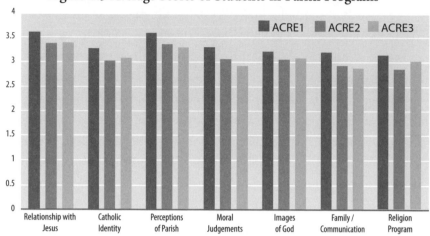

Figure 2.5 Average Scores of Students in Parish Programs

Chapter 3
Faith Knowledge: Domains 1 to 4

This chapter contains the analysis of the first four domains of faith knowledge: God, Church, Liturgy and Sacraments, and Revelation, Scripture and Faith. The tables and figures in this chapter display the percentage of Catholic students from Catholic schools and those from parish religious education programs who answered the items correctly. The scores of non-Catholic students in Catholic schools are omitted from these and subsequent analyses in the book since the intention is to focus on the performance of Catholic students. In presenting information about incorrect responses, only those responses that were selected by more than 10 percent of students either in Catholic schools or in parish programs are reported.

Domain 1
God: Father, Son and Holy Spirit

The items in Domain 1 explore the students' understanding of the Church's teaching about the Trinity and the role and nature of each Person in the Trinity. The content of these items generally concern matters of defined dogma. Some items in this domain also explore understanding of the public life of Jesus, the Nicene Creed and the gifts of the Holy Spirit.

Key Objective

Know and understand basic Catholic teaching about God as Father, Son, and Holy Spirit

Key Concepts

Trinity, God the Father, God the Son, God the Holy Spirit, Creed, God's activity in human history

Table 3.1 presents the summary statistics for Domain 1, God – Father, Son and Holy Spirit. On average, across the three levels of ACRE, Catholic students in Catholic schools correctly answered 82 percent of the items and students from parish religious education programs correctly answered 71 percent of the items. The greatest difference between the performance of students in Catholic schools and those in parish programs occurred on ACRE2, which is the only level of ACRE on which a large effect size occurs (.72). The effect sizes for ACRE1 and ACRE3 are both in the medium range. The overall percent correct in this domain declined slightly from ACRE1 to ACRE3.

Table 3.1 ACRE Results: 2004-2005
Domain 1: God-Father, Son and Holy Spirit

	Catholics in Catholic School	Catholics in Parish Programs	Total	Effect Size
ACRE1 (6 items)				
Percent Correct	84%	74%	82%	
Mean	5.05	4.41	4.92	.58
SD	1.05	1.21	1.11	
ACRE2 (7 items)				
Percent Correct	82%	68%	79%	
Mean	5.75	4.77	5.56	.72
SD	1.27	1.48	1.37	
ACRE3 (8 items)				
Percent Correct	79%	70%	78%	
Mean	6.36	5.59	6.20	.44
SD	1.70	1.85	1.77	

ACRE1

Catholic students in both Catholic schools and parish programs who took ACRE1 generally understood Jesus' divine and human nature, His role in salvation, how He addressed God as Father, and why it is important to honor Mary (Figure 3.1).

On the other hand, the students showed less understanding of the Holy Spirit as the third Person of the Trinity and the role of the Spirit in the Church.

Just over two-thirds of those in Catholic schools and just over one-half of those in parish programs answered these items correctly. A number of students, especially those in parish programs, identified the Holy Spirit as the Son of God (22% in parish programs) or as the redeemer of the world (13% in parish programs).

Seventy percent of the students in Catholic schools and just over half of the students in parish programs correctly answered that Jesus promised to send the Spirit as a continued presence in the Church. However, a significant number of students incorrectly answered that, rather than the Holy Spirit, Jesus promised to send saints (26% in parish programs, 14% in Catholic schools) or peacemakers (13% in parish programs, 11% in Catholic schools) to be present in the Church.

Figure 3.1 ACRE1- God: Father, Son and Holy Spirit

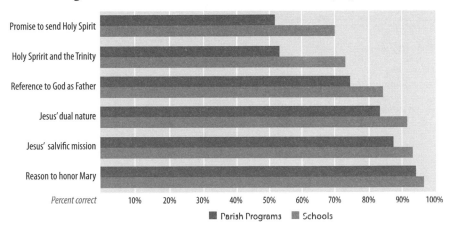

ACRE2

The Catholic students who took ACRE2 demonstrated good understanding of Jesus' salvific role, His nature as divine and human, the Spirit's work in the world, and the proclamation of the kingdom of God as the central theme of Jesus' mission (Figure 3.2).

Just over three-quarters of the students in Catholic schools and just over half of those in parish programs correctly answered that each person in the

Trinity is fully God. On the other hand, 21 percent of Catholic school students and 39 percent of those in parish program incorrectly thought that the three persons of the Trinity represent three Gods. Other misconceptions were that the acts of faith, hope, and charity (19% in Catholic schools, 34% in parish programs), rather than the Nicene Creed, contained a summary of the essential beliefs of Catholicism, and that the Immaculate Conception (18% in Catholic schools, 28% in parish programs) or the birth of Jesus (19% in Catholic schools, 23% in parish programs), rather than the Trinity, constituted the central mystery of Christian faith.

Figure 3.2 ACRE2 - God: Father, Son and Holy Spirit

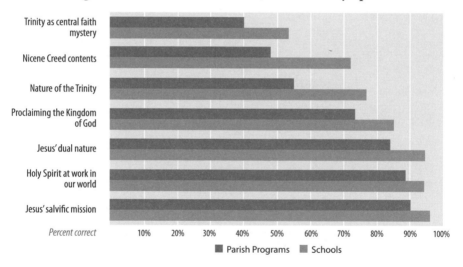

ACRE3

The high school students on ACRE3 showed an adequate understanding on six of the eight items in this domain (Figure 3.3). The students understood the centrality of Jesus' death and resurrection, God as the source of creation and still active in the world, and Jesus welcoming sinners during his public ministry. In addition, a large majority correctly identified wisdom and courage as gifts of the Holy Spirit, each person in the Trinity as fully God, and Jesus as truly God and truly man. However, one-fifth to a quarter of the students in parish programs had misconceptions about these truths, choosing liberation and acceptance as gifts of the Holy Spirit (20% in parish programs), the Trinity as representing three Gods (25% in parish programs), and Jesus as a man who became God (20% in parish programs).

Students from both Catholic schools and parish programs demonstrated less understanding on two items, the communion of saints and the Nicene Creed. Only two-thirds of the Catholic school students and just over a half of those in parish programs answered these items correctly. The major misconception about the communion of saints was that it includes only those in heaven (22% in Catholic schools, 27% in parish programs). When asked to identify the prayer that expresses the Church's belief that Jesus is one with God, 21 percent of Catholic school students and 25 percent of those in parish programs answered the Lord's Prayer, rather than the Nicene Creed.

Figure 3.3 ACRE3 - God: Father, Son and Holy Spirit

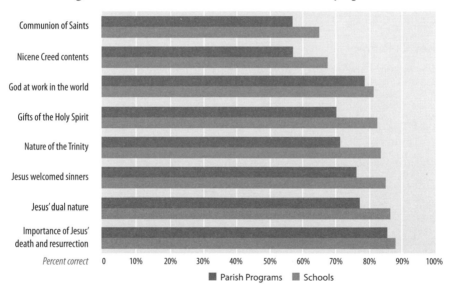

Summary

The overall performance of students on Domain 1 was generally good with 82 percent of students (84% of those in Catholic schools and 74% of those in parish programs) answering items correctly. Areas of strength include understanding of Jesus' dual nature and his role in salvation (ACRE1, ACRE2, and ACRE3), the importance of Mary in the Church (ACRE1), the understanding that the kingdom of God is a central theme of Jesus' mission (ACRE3), and the nature of the gifts of the Holy Spirit (ACRE3).

Some areas of weakness involve students' understanding of the person and role of the Holy Spirit, the nature of the Trinity as a central mystery of the faith, the Nicene Creed and its significance, and the nature of the communion of saints.

Domain 2
Church: One, Holy, Catholic, and Apostolic

The items in Domain 2 concern the four characteristics or marks of the Church, with specific reference to Mary's role in the Church, how the Church is organized and governed, its evangelization mission, the role of the parish, and the understanding of the communion of saints.

Key Objective

Understand the origin, mission, structure, community and membership of the Church

Key Concepts

Attributes of the Church, Mary, Church as the People of God, Body of Christ, communion of saints, role of Church leaders, ecumenism, Church's mission and evangelization, Church as community

Table 3.2 contains the summary statistics for Domain 2, the Church – One, Holy, Catholic and Apostolic. On average, across the three levels of ACRE, Catholic school students answered 78 percent of the items correctly and students from parish religious education programs answered 68 percent correctly. The greatest difference between the performance of students in Catholic schools and those in parish programs once again occurred on ACRE2, which is the only level in which a large effect size occurred (.76). The effect size for ACRE1 is in the medium range (.49) and that for ACRE3 in the small range (.21). The students who took ACRE 3 performed slightly better in this domain than those who took ACRE1 and ACRE2.

Table 3.2 ACRE Results: 2004-2005
Domain 2: Church-One, Holy, Catholic, and Apostolic

	Catholics in Catholic School	Catholics in Parish Programs	Total	Effect Size
ACRE1 (5 items)				
Percent Correct	77%	67%	75%	
Mean	3.86	3.33	3.75	.49
SD	1.04	1.10	1.08	
ACRE2 (8 items)				
Percent Correct	75%	59%	72%	
Mean	6.03	4.73	5.79	.76
SD	1.60	1.80	1.72	
ACRE3 (8 items)				
Percent Correct	82%	77%	80%	
Mean	6.54	6.19	6.43	.21
SD	1.55	1.67	1.63	

ACRE1

Most Catholic students who took ACRE1 understood that Mary is the Mother of the Church and that parishes care for the poor to fulfill Jesus' commandment to love our neighbor (Figure 3.4). Most also correctly answered that all baptized are called to share their faith; however, a number of students thought that all baptized are called to go to Mass daily (16% in Catholic schools, 29% in parish programs).

Figure 3.4 ACRE1 - Church: One, Holy, Catholic and Apostolic

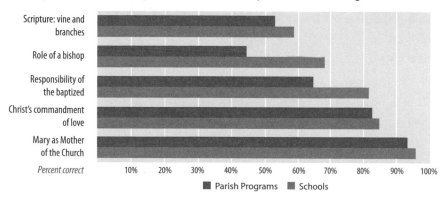

One-third of the Catholic school students and more than half of those in parish programs failed to identify a diocese as the organizational unit headed by a cardinal or bishop. Those who answered incorrectly thought that the bishop was in charge of a province (11% in Catholic schools, 28% in parish programs), a state (11% in Catholic schools, 15% in parish programs) or a city (13% in parish programs).

Almost half of the students also had trouble correctly identifying "I am the vine and you are the branches" as an appropriate scriptural reference that describes Jesus' relationship with the Church. The most commonly selected incorrect response was "come follow me" (15% in Catholic schools, 23% in parish programs), followed by "repent and believe the good news" (12% in Catholic schools, 14% in parish programs) and "let the children come to me" (11% in Catholic schools, 11% in parish programs). The symbolism of the biblical passage was missed by almost half of the students who took ACRE1. Perhaps, the expectation that 10- or 11-year old students would recognize this passage as describing Jesus' relationship with his Church was unrealistic.

ACRE2

The students who took ACRE2 showed good understanding of the importance of Mary and the teaching authority of the pope united with the bishops (Figure 3.5). Most in Catholic schools (80%) understood that the missionary aspect of the Church implies that Catholic share the good news with others; however, a significant number in parish programs (27%) thought it meant that Catholics must support their parish. Approximately seven of ten students correctly answered that lay people participate in evangelization through good example and good works, and that active involvement in the parish is the responsibility of all who are baptized.

Most students in Catholic schools (75%) understood that the term "catholic" means universal, while less than half of those in parish programs had that understanding. Most students who answered incorrectly thought that catholic meant saintly (16% in Catholic schools, 35% in parish programs).

Figure 3.5 ACRE2 - Church: One, Holy, Catholic and Apostolic

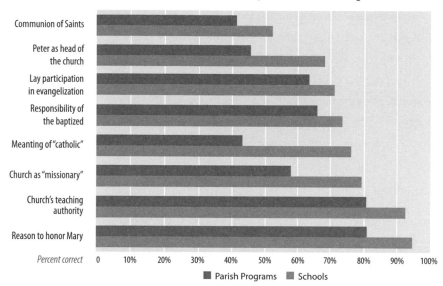

About two-thirds of the Catholic school students (69%), but less than half of those in parish programs (45%), knew that Peter was the first head of the Church. Students in parish programs alternatively selected the other available choices: John (22%), Moses (18%) or Paul (16%).

Only about half of the students (52% in Catholic schools, 41% in parish programs) had a proper understanding of the communion of saints as "the union of believers, living and dead, who form one body in Christ." However, some thought that the term referred to canonized saints (25% in Catholic schools, 25% in parish programs) or those already in heaven (18% in Catholic schools, 21% in parish programs).

ACRE3

Generally, the high school students who took ACRE3, both in Catholic schools and parish programs, showed more understanding of the Church and its characteristics than the younger students did, with the average score for all students exceeding 80 percent correct on four items and, for those in Catholic schools, on a fifth item as well (Figure 3.6). About a third of the students failed to recognize the truth of the statement that the Church's teaching is a sure voice to guide us through life, picking instead that the Church and the kingdom of God are the same (32% in Catholic schools, 29% in parish programs). Other misconceptions included selecting as true statements that the Church's call to evangelize means to serve the needs of all people (14% in Catholic schools, 19% in parish programs) and that the mission of the Church is the responsibility of the pope and the bishops (13% in Catholic schools, 16% in parish programs), rather than all baptized Catholics.

Figure 3.6 ACRE3 - Church: One, Holy, Catholic and Apostolic

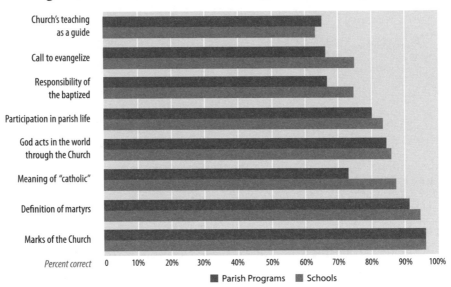

Summary

The overall performance of the students on Domain 2 was slightly lower than their performance on Domain 1. Areas of strength include understanding of Mary's role in the Church (ACRE1, ACRE2), the responsibilities of the baptized, the importance of the teaching authority of the Pope and the Church (ACRE2), the responsibilities of the baptized (ACRE2), the Marks or Characteristics of the Church (ACRE3), and the importance of parish life (ACRE3).

Some areas of weakness involve failure to recognize symbolism of the Church in Scripture (ACRE1), the roles of bishops (ACRE1), understanding of the broad meaning of catholic (ACRE2), the nature of the communion of saints (ACRE2), recognition that Peter was the first head of the Church (ACRE2), and equating the Church and the kingdom of God (ACRE3).

It should be noted that an item concerning the communion of saints is in this domain on ACRE2 and while a similar item on the same concept with different wording appears on ACRE3 in Domain 1. This raises the question about the appropriate domain placement of the concept of the communion of saints that should be resolved in future revisions of ACRE. In both cases, between 30 and 40 percent of the students thought the term referred to those who are in heaven or who have been canonized as saints.

Domain 3
Liturgy and Sacraments

The items in Domain 3 assess the students' understanding of the sacraments, the Mass, the liturgical year and liturgical symbols.

Key Objectives
1. Know about Church's liturgical life in terms of liturgical feasts, seasons, symbols, religious practices and concepts of prayer
2. Know and understand the sacraments as signs and instruments of grace

Key Concepts
Liturgical year, liturgical symbols, Mass, role in the liturgy, celebration of sacraments as signs of grace and encounters with Christ, Sacraments of Initiation, Healing, and Vocation

Table 3.3 ACRE Results: 2004-2005
Domain 3: Liturgy and Sacraments

	Catholics in Catholic School	Catholics in Parish Programs	Total	Effect Size
ACRE1 (9 items)				
Percent Correct	75%	62%	72%	
Mean	6.75	5.56	6.48	.61
SD	1.84	1.98	1.94	
ACRE2 (8 items)				
Percent Correct	74%	60%	71%	
Mean	5.88	4.81	5.66	.63
SD	1.62	1.75	1.71	
ACRE3 (7 items)				
Percent Correct	77%	72%	75%	
Mean	5.38	5.02	5.23	.23
SD	1.48	1.56	1.57	

Table 3.3 presents the summary statistics for the third domain of Faith Knowledge: Liturgy and Sacraments. On average, across the three levels of ACRE, Catholic school students answered 75 percent of the items correctly and students from parish religious education programs answered 65 percent correctly. The effect sizes for ACRE1 (.61) and ACRE2 (.63) are in the medium range and that for ACRE3 is in the small range (.23).

ACRE1

The students who took ACRE1 generally showed adequate to very good understanding of the sacraments (Figure 3.7). Over 90 percent in both Catholic schools and parish programs knew that the Eucharist is Jesus' Body and Blood. Between 70 percent and 85 percent of those in Catholic schools understood the nature of sacraments, recognized the purpose of Penance and Holy Orders, and correctly identified Baptism as a sacrament of initiation. On the other hand, the performance of students in parish programs on these same items was somewhat lower, ranging from 60 percent to 67 percent correct. The most common misconceptions were that the sacraments were required by the Ten Commandments (15% in Catholic schools, 23% in parish programs) or that the prophets talked about them (11% in Catholic schools, 15% in parish programs).

Figure 3.7 ACRE1 - Liturgy and Sacraments

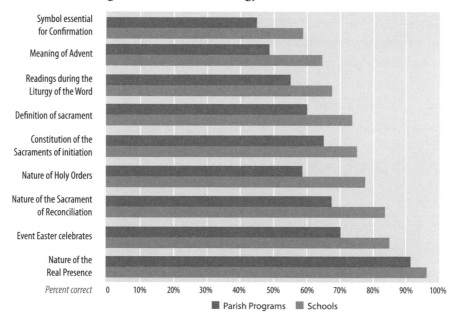

A number of students from parish programs also misidentified the Anointing of the Sick (13% in parish programs), Matrimony (12% in parish programs), and Holy Orders (11% in parish programs) as Sacraments of Initiation. In addition, some from parish programs thought that the sacrament associated with ordination was the Eucharist (15% in parish programs), Matrimony (11% in parish programs) or Penance (11% in parish programs).

With the exception of the association of Easter Sunday with Jesus' resurrection (82% in Catholic schools, 70% in parish programs), the overall performance of the students on the items pertaining to the liturgy was poorer than their performance on the sacramental items. The range of correct scores on the items pertaining to the liturgy was 59 percent to 67 percent for Catholic school students and 45 percent to 55 percent for students from parish programs. In identifying the part of the Mass a lector might read from the Old Testament, 67 percent of Catholic school students and 55 percent of students in parish programs correctly answered the Liturgy of the Word, while 20 percent of Catholic school students and 24 percent of those in parish programs incorrectly answered the Gospel. A significant number of students (26% in Catholic schools, 34% in parish programs) misidentified the meaning of Advent, indicating that it was the season that prepares the Church for Easter.

Finally, the item with which the students had the most trouble was the liturgical symbol essential to Confirmation. Fifty-nine percent of Catholic school students and 45 percent of those in parish programs correctly identified the oil of Chrism. Other students incorrectly selected the candle (21% in Catholic schools, 26% in parish programs), the white garment (12% in Catholic schools, 15% in parish programs), or water (13% in parish programs)

ACRE2

The students on ACRE2 generally correctly identified that Holy Thursday commemorates the Last Supper; that Baptism, Confirmation and Eucharist are Sacraments of Initiation; and the reasons for celebrating the sacraments (Figure 3.8). Most students understood that Holy Orders is the sacrament that gives bishops, priests and deacons the power to minister to the Christian community and that the Mass is the most important act of worship for Catholics. About two-thirds of Catholic students in Catholic schools, but slightly less than half of those in parish programs, knew that green is the liturgical color for Ordinary Time and that the Ascension is the feast on which Catholics celebrate Jesus' going to heaven.

On the other hand, the students showed substantial lack of knowledge and/or understanding of the term "transubstantiation." Less than half of the students in Catholic schools and about one-third of those in parish programs recognized transubstantiation as the name of the doctrine that refers to the Real Presence in the Eucharist.

Figure 3.8 ACRE2 - Liturgy and Sacraments

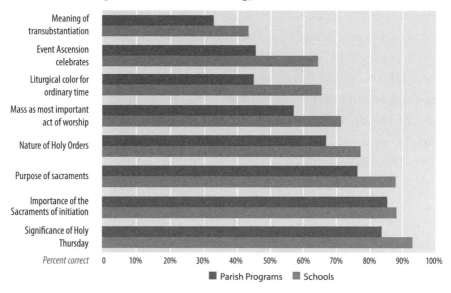

The major misconceptions on this domain for those who took ACRE2 were:

- Identifying the feast that celebrates Jesus going to heaven as the Resurrection (24% in Catholic schools, 35% in parish programs) or the Assumption (10% in Catholic schools, 15% in parish programs);

- Identifying the doctrine of the real presence of Jesus in the Eucharist as Transfiguration (33% in Catholic schools, 31% in parish programs) or Incarnation (16% in Catholic schools, 26% in parish programs);

- Selecting white (18% in Catholic schools, 27% in parish programs) or purple (13% in Catholic schools, 23% in parish programs) as the color for Ordinary Time.

- Selecting the Rite of Reconciliation as the most important act of worship in the Catholic community (14% in Catholic schools, 21% in parish programs).

ACRE3

The students in Catholic schools and parish programs who took ACRE3 had a good understanding of the sacraments, some misunderstanding of the nature of the liturgical year and a major misconception of the meaning of the Immaculate Conception (Figure 3.9). A large majority knew the purpose of a sacrament, the nature of Holy Communion and the sacrament of marriage, and recognized the Mass as the most important act of worship for Catholics and Holy Orders as the sacrament received by priests at ordination. Most (70% in Catholic schools, 65% in parish programs) also correctly identified the duration of the liturgical year; however, some thought the liturgical year is simply the period from Ash Wednesday to Easter (16% in Catholic schools, 19% in parish programs).

Figure 3.9 ACRE3 - Liturgy and Sacraments

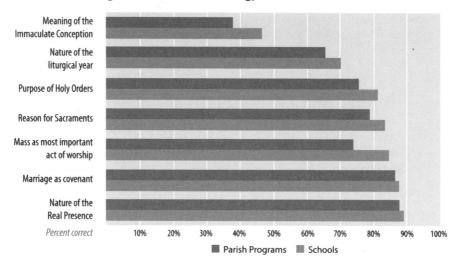

The biggest misconception on ACRE3 concerned the understanding of the Immaculate Conception. Less than half (46% in Catholic schools, 37% in parish programs) knew that the feast of the Immaculate Conception celebrates Mary's freedom from original sin. An almost equal number (40% in Catholic schools, 41% in parish programs) incorrectly answered that the feast of the Immaculate Conception celebrates Mary's virginity.

Summary

The overall performance of the students regarding the items on Liturgy and

Sacrament was lower than their performance on items referring to God (Domain 1) and the Church (Domain 2). Areas of strength include basic understanding of the sacraments (ACRE1, ACRE2, and ACRE3), understanding of the importance of Holy Thursday (ACRE2), and some knowledge of the liturgical year (ACRE3).

Areas of weakness include understanding the liturgy and its components (ACRE1), the nature of Holy Orders (ACRE1), the meaning of Advent (ACRE1) and of transubstantiation (ACRE2), and the failure to recognize the Mass as the most important act of worship in the Church (ACRE2).

Substantial confusion also exists about the meaning of the mysteries celebrated by the major feast days of the Church, the Resurrection, Assumption, Ascension, and Immaculate Conception. Another area of weakness on ACRE1 was failure to recognize the oil of Chrism as the essential liturgical symbol for Confirmation. In most dioceses, children are confirmed later than the 5th or 6th grade, so it is not surprising that students would not know the correct answer since the fundamental catechesis about it likely doesn't occur by that grade.

Domain 4
Revelation, Scripture and Faith

The items in Domain 4 explore the students' understanding of scripture as God's inspired word and their understanding of the nature of revelation, primarily through scripture.

Key Objectives

1. Recognize Scripture as God's inspired word
2. Know the major divisions of the Bible, the chief persons in biblical history, and major biblical themes from the Old and New Testaments

Key Concepts

- The Bible as the inspired Word of God, parts of the Bible and Gospel writers

- Major biblical themes of the Old Testament: creation, sin, covenant, Exodus, law, prophets, Kingdom

- Major biblical themes of the New Testament: parables, miracles, Kingdom of God, beatitudes, paschal mystery, Jesus' mission, eternal hope

- Responses to God's call

Table 3.4 ACRE Results: 2004-2005
Domain 4: Revelation, Scripture and Faith

	Catholics in Catholic School	Catholics in Parish Programs	Total	Effect Size
ACRE1 (9 items)				
Percent Correct	82%	71%	80%	
Mean	5.76	4.95	5.60	.58
SD	1.31	1.51	1.39	
ACRE2 (8 items)				
Percent Correct	79%	62%	76%	
Mean	4.75	3.70	4.57	.74
SD	1.32	1.51	1.41	
ACRE3 (7 items)				
Percent Correct	63%	50%	61%	
Mean	5.04	3.96	4.90	.56
SD	1.92	1.78	1.94	

Table 3.4 presents the summary statistics for the domain: Revelation, Scripture and Faith. On average, Catholic school students answered 75 percent of the items correctly and students from parish religious education programs answered 61 percent correctly, making the performance on this domain similar to that on Domain 3, Liturgy and Sacraments. The effect size for ACRE2 (.74) is once again in the large range, while the effect sizes for ACRE1 (.58) and ACRE3 (.56) are in the medium range.

ACRE1

Most students, particularly those in Catholic schools, generally showed very good understanding of the items on ACRE1 pertaining to revelation and scripture

(Figure 3.10). The majority of students knew the nature of the Bible, the definition of the Trinity, the scripture stories of the Prodigal Son and the Good Samaritan, the meaning of the verse "Whatever you did for one of these least brothers of mine, you did for me," and that the Gospels tell us most about the life and work of Jesus. A sizeable number, however, thought that stories about Jesus, Mary and the Apostles are found in the Old Testament (27% in Catholic schools, 40% in parish programs).

Figure 3.10 ACRE1 - Revelation, Scripture and Faith

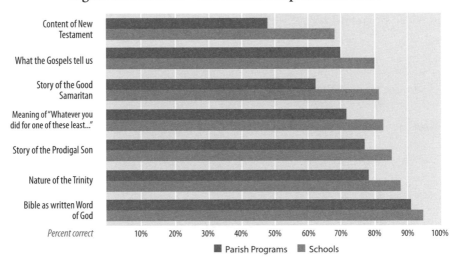

ACRE2

Most students on ACRE2 correctly identified the nature of discipleship, the lesson in the Gospel story of the Prodigal Son, Abraham as the father of God's chosen people, and the definition of covenant as used in the Old Testament (Figure 3.11). Some, however, answered that David was the father of God's chosen people (12% in Catholic schools, 24% in parish programs) and that God's promise of partnership made with Moses was called prophecy (24% in parish programs) or prayer (11% in parish programs).

Many students did not understand what the Church means by Tradition. When asked to identify the term that describes the beliefs and practices in the Church that are passed down from one generation to the next under the guidance of the Holy Spirit, 72 percent of students in Catholic schools and 55 percent of those in parish programs correctly identified Tradition. On the other hand, some thought that the correct term is sacraments (12% in Catholic schools, 20% in parish programs) or rituals (14% in Catholic schools, 19% in parish programs).

Still more students did not understand the nature of the Paschal Mystery. Some selected responses that the Paschal Mystery refers to what happens after death (13% in Catholic schools, 27% in parish programs), Jesus' birth, baptism and temptation in the desert (12% in Catholic schools, 15% in parish programs) or the Trinity (14% in parish programs).

Figure 3.11 ACRE2 - Revelation, Scripture and Faith

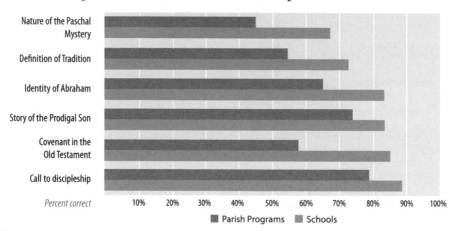

ACRE3

The items regarding Revelation, Scripture and Faith on ACRE3 (Figure 3.12) proved to be more difficult than those on ACRE1 and ACRE2. Most (73%) in Catholic schools understood the meaning of the Bible as the inspired word of God; however, just over half (51%) in parish programs answered the item correctly. The students in parish programs who answered incorrectly interpreted the inspired word as historically accurate accounts (21%), inspirational reading (16%) or dictation by God (12%).

The students on ACRE3 did slightly better on the understanding of the Paschal Mystery than did those who took ACRE2. Misconceptions persisted, however, with some indicating that the Paschal Mystery refers to what happens after death (27% in parish programs), Jesus' birth, baptism and temptation in the desert (11% in Catholic schools, 14% in parish programs) or the Trinity (12% in parish programs).

Many high-school-age students did not know when the Gospels were written. Correct answers were given by 62 percent of Catholic school students and just 47 percent of those in parish programs. Some thought the Gospels were written while Jesus was alive (14% in Catholic schools, 28% in parish programs), as eye-witness accounts by reporters (11% in Catholic schools, 13% in parish programs) or during the third and fourth centuries by later believers (14% in Catholic schools, 13% in parish programs).

Approximately six in ten high school students knew that the Acts of the Apostles told the story of the faith and struggles of the early Church, but about one-third (30% in Catholic schools, 36% in parish programs) incorrectly thought the Acts told the story of Jesus' birth, death and resurrection.

Figure 3.12 ACRE3 - Revelation, Scripture and Faith

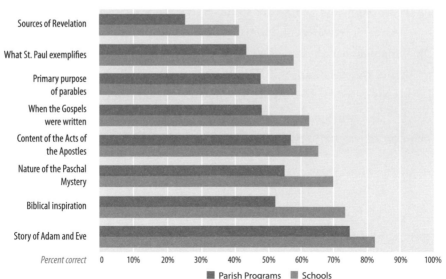

When asked to identify the person in the New Testament who exemplified a faithful response to God's call through his letters and travels, only 58 percent of Catholic school students and 43 percent of those in parish programs correctly named Paul. Others selected Matthew (19% in Catholic schools, 25% in parish programs), Mark (16% in Catholic schools, 22% in parish programs) or Lazarus (11% in parish programs).

The poorest performance of the students on ACRE3 came in their understanding that Tradition is a source of revelation in addition to Sacred Scripture. Only 41 percent of those in Catholic schools and one-fourth of those in parish programs correctly identified Tradition as a source of revelation. The most common misconceptions of the source of revelation in addition to scripture were prophecy (33% in Catholic schools, 44% in parish programs) and virtue (17% in Catholic schools, 21% in parish programs).

Summary

The areas of strength on Domain 4 include understanding of the Bible as the inspired word of God (ACRE1, ACRE3 for students in Catholic schools), familiarity with popular Bible stories (ACRE1, ACRE2), the nature of the Gospels (ACRE1), the nature of the Trinity (ACRE1), and understanding of the covenant (ACRE2 for students in Catholic schools).

Areas of weakness on Domain 4 include confusing the content of the Old Testament and the New Testament (ACRE1), understanding of Tradition as a source of revelation (ACRE2, ACRE3), understanding the nature of the Paschal Mystery (ACRE2, ACRE3), knowing when the Gospels were written (ACRE3), knowing the primary purpose of parables (ACRE3), and recognizing the importance of St. Paul in the scriptures (ACRE3).

Chapter 4
Faith Knowledge: Domains 5 to 8

This chapter contains the analysis of the second four domains of faith knowledge: Personal Morality and Catholic Social Teaching, Church History, Prayer/Religious Practice and Catholic Faith Literacy. As in Chapter 3, the tables and figures in this chapter display the mean scores, standard deviations, effect sizes, and percentage of Catholic students from Catholic schools and those from parish religious education programs who answered the items correctly. The scores of non-Catholic students in Catholic schools are omitted from these analyses. In presenting information about incorrect responses, only those responses that were selected by more than 10 percent of students either in Catholic schools or in parish programs are reported.

Domain 5
Life in Christ: Personal Morality and Catholic Social Teaching

The items in Domain 5 assess the students' understanding of the basis for Christian morality, Catholic social teaching, the nature of sin, and the importance of a well-formed conscience for decision-making.

Key Objectives

1. Know the teachings of Jesus and the Church as the basis of Christian morality and understand Catholic Social Teaching
2. Be aware of the importance of a well-formed conscience for decision-making

Key Concepts

- Beatitudes and Ten Commandments; theological virtues, ongoing conversion, personal and social aspects of sin;

- Seven principles of Catholic Social Teaching: life and dignity of the human person; call to family, community and participation; rights and responsibilities; preferential option for the poor and vulnerable; dignity of work and rights of workers; solidarity; care for God's creation

- Conscience; morality as based on natural and divine law

Table 4.1 presents the summary statistics for the domain: Life in Christ – Personal Morality and Catholic Social Teachings. On average, Catholic school students answered 69 percent of the items correctly and students from parish religious education programs answered 61 percent correctly. The magnitude of the differences between the performance of students in Catholic schools and those in parish programs is in the medium range for ACRE1 (.52) and ACRE2 (.57), and in the small range for ACRE3 (.23). Overall, the items in this domain were among the most challenging for the students at each level of ACRE.

Table 4.1 ACRE Results: 2004-2005
Domain 5: Life in Christ – Personal Morality and Catholic Social Teachings

	Catholics in Catholic School	Catholics in Parish Programs	Total	Effect Size
ACRE1 (7 items)				
Percent Correct	65%	55%	63%	
Mean	4.55	3.84	4.41	.52
SD	1.32	1.45	1.37	
ACRE2 (10 items)				
Percent Correct	80%	69%	78%	
Mean	7.98	6.86	7.76	.57
SD	1.82	2.23	1.96	
ACRE3 (10 items)				
Percent Correct	63%	58%	62%	
Mean	6.33	5.84	6.24	.23
SD	2.05	2.08	2.10	

ACRE1

For the most part, the students who took ACRE1 demonstrated good understanding of Catholic social teaching pertaining to protecting the environment and good understanding of the meaning and structure of the Ten Commandments (Figure 4.1). The common misconceptions that emerged were that Jesus gave the Ten Commandments to his disciples on Mt. Sinai (12% in Catholic schools, 20% in parish programs) or that the first five commandments are about loving the Church and the last five are about loving God (11% in Catholic schools, 19% in parish programs).

Just over three-fourths of those in Catholic schools and just over half in parish programs knew that Jesus gave the Beatitudes in the Sermon on the Mount. Those who answered incorrectly identified the lessons that Jesus gave in the Sermon on the Mount as the laws of the Church (10% in Catholic schools, 17% in parish programs), the gifts of the Holy Spirit (16% in parish programs) or the epistles (12% in parish programs).

This domain contained a very difficult item for the fifth graders regarding the theological virtue of hope. Only 10 percent of Catholic school students and 12 percent of those in parish programs correctly identified hope as the virtue that helps us trust God's promises even when it is difficult to do so. The vast majority of students (71% in Catholic schools, 61% in parish programs) selected faith as the virtue that helps us trust God's promises. For young people, the distinction between faith and hope is often difficult to make. In common parlance, young people tend to equate "I trust you" with "I have faith in you." Thus, it is not surprising that a very high number of students chose the faith response. Some even selected love, the option that was available as opposed to charity, as the virtue that helps us trust God's promises (16% in Catholic schools, 24% in parish programs).

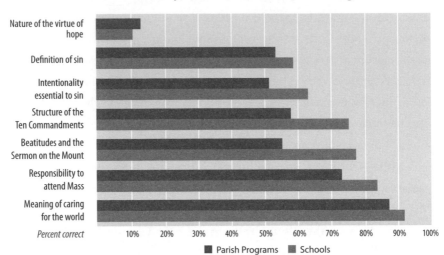

Figure 4.1 ACRE1 - Life in Christ:
Personal Morality and Catholic Social Teaching

Many students who took ACRE1 did not have a good understanding of sin. Slightly more than half correctly identified sin as a choice to do something they know offends God. A significant number, however, identified sin as choosing something wrong by accident (15% in Catholic schools, 22% in parish programs) or choosing to do something that other people do not like (16% in Catholic schools, 19% in parish programs). In responding to a second item concerning sin, more than half correctly identified personal sin as words, utterances, actions or desires contrary to God's law; however, a significant number of students saw sin as making a mistake (21% in Catholic schools, 25% in parish programs) or accidentally hurting someone (14% in Catholic schools, 14% in parish programs).

ACRE2

Compared with students who took ACRE1, the students on ACRE2 performed about the same or better on items pertaining to Catholic social justice and the understanding of the commandments and personal sin (Figure 4.2). Those who took ACRE2, however, also continued to have a problem with the understanding of the theological virtues, in this case, the virtue of faith. When asked to define the theological virtue of faith, fewer than half of the students answered that faith is a gift by which we believe in God and all that God has revealed. The misconceptions about faith included choosing the response that faith is "a virtue by which we trust (note the use of "trust" again in a distracter) in God's promise of eternal life" (38% in Catholic schools, 37% in parish programs) or "the way we practice our religion" (16% in parish programs).

Finally, most students who took ACRE2 understood that in accord with Catholic teaching life begins at conception. A significant number, however, incorrectly selected that life begins at birth (23% in Catholic schools, 38% in parish programs).

Figure 4.2 ACRE2 - Life in Christ:
Personal Morality and Catholic Social Teaching

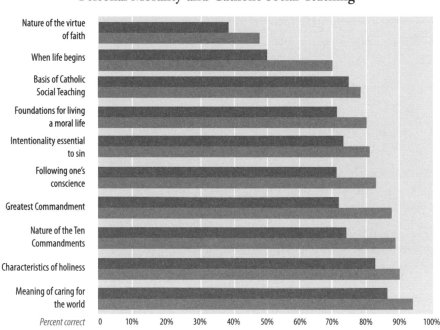

ACRE3

The students who took ACRE3 demonstrated good understanding of the Catholic perspective on AIDS, the nature of sin, and the basis for Catholic social teaching (Figure 4.3). The vast majority (87% in Catholic schools and 85% in parish programs) also correctly answered the item that asked about the nature of the theological virtue of hope; however, it should be noted that none of the distracters for this item on ACRE3 contained the word "trust," which was likely the source of the problem for the students on ACRE1, making this item on its face easier than the item about hope on ACRE1. Of course, a contributing factor to the better performance of the high school students compared to the performance of students who took ACRE1 is that the former students had a better understanding of hope than did the latter students.

The performance by students in both Catholic schools and parish programs was unsatisfactory (less than 60 percent correct) on items pertaining to conscience and individual freedom (2 items), universal moral laws, the Church's teaching authority on faith and morals, and the meanings of moral conversion and "a preferential option for the poor."

The observed misconceptions of the high school students about these issues were:

- Conscience is based on what a person feels is right or wrong (27% in Catholic schools, 27% in parish programs);

- True freedom means deciding for one's self what is good and evil (52% in Catholic schools, 49% in parish programs);

- There are no universal moral laws (10% in Catholic schools, 12% in parish programs) or people create their own morality by free choice (26% in Catholic schools, 28% in parish programs);

- Rather than the Church's Magisterium teaching on faith and morals, the local bishops reveal new truths (22% in Catholic schools, 24% in parish programs) or Catholic teachings do not change (13% in Catholic schools, 19% in parish programs) or the people are free to accept dogmas with which they agree and ignore the rest (10% in Catholic schools, 12% in parish programs);

- Rather than a concern for the powerless, a consequence of moral conversion is having an attitude to "live and let live" (25% in Catholic schools, 26% in parish programs) or seeking others' approval for doing God's will (21% in Catholic schools, 24% in parish programs) or believing you have no further need to change (16% in Catholic schools, 16% in parish programs);

- Rather than giving careful consideration to the impact of decisions on the poor, a "preferential option for the poor" means that charitable organizations should try to take care of the needs of the poor (36% in Catholic schools, 41% in parish programs) or give preference to the poor for available jobs (15% in Catholic schools, 15% in parish programs).

Figure 4.3 ACRE3 - Life in Christ:
Personal Morality and Catholic Social Teaching

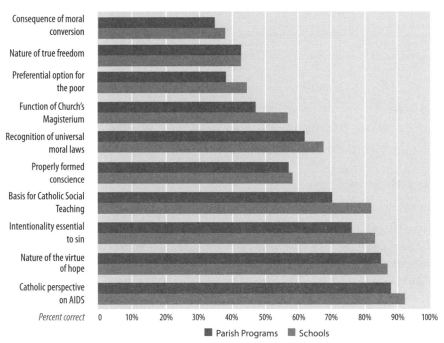

Summary

In a departure from the previous domains, the performance of students on ACRE2, particularly those in Catholic schools, was the best on this domain. Areas of strength include a good understanding of Catholic Social Teaching (ACRE1, ACRE2, and ACRE3), the meaning and structure of the Ten Commandments (ACRE1), and, for the high school students on ACRE3, a proper understanding of sin and understanding of the Catholic perspective on AIDS.

Areas of weakness in this domain include a lack of understanding of the theological virtues of faith and hope (ACRE1, ACRE2), the nature of sin (ACRE1), when life begins (ACRE2 for students in parish programs), the meaning of the Magisterium (ACRE3), the Church's teaching authority on faith and morals (ACRE3), proper understanding of conscience and freedom (ACRE3), and the meaning of preferential option for the poor (ACRE3).

Domain 6
Church History

The Church History domain contains a variety of items and its content differs somewhat across the levels of ACRE. The primary objective of this domain is to test the students' familiarity with key events and major figures that have shaped the history of the Church.

Key Objective

Become familiar with the central stories, key events and major figures that have shaped the history and development of the Church overtime as appropriate for the student's grade level

Key Concepts

- Apostolic age: Pentecost and formation of Scripture;
- 4th century: end of persecution, Nicene Creed, Catechumenate, Mary as Mother of God;
- 11th century: St. Francis of Assisi, St. Clare of Assisi, devotional life, reform of church;
- 16th century: Reformation and Council of Trent, St. Ignatius Loyola, St. Theresa of Avila, missionary movement;

- 18th century: Age of Enlightenment, French revolution, immigration and Church in America, Bishop Carroll, Mother Seton, Kateri Tekakwitha;

- 19th century: Church and worker, Leo XIII and Rerum Novarum, Catholic Social Teaching;

- 20th century: Pius X and age of communion, US church and immigrants, restoration of the Catechumenate, Vatican II, ecumenism, Pope John Paul II, St. Katharine Drexel, Archbishop Oscar Romero, Dorothy Day.

Table 4.2 contains the summary statistics for the Church History domain. On average, Catholic school students answered 63 percent of the items correctly and students from parish religious education programs answered 48 percent correctly. A very large difference (effect size = .84) occurs between the performance of students in Catholic schools and those in parish programs on ACRE2. The difference between the performance of students in Catholic schools and those in parish programs is in the medium range for ACRE1 (.50) and ACRE3 (.37).

Table 4.2 ACRE Results: 2004-2005
Domain 6: Church History

	Catholics in Catholic School	Catholics in Parish Programs	Total	Effect Size
ACRE1 (4 items)				
Percent Correct	64%	50%	61%	
Mean	2.55	1.99	2.43	.50
SD	1.08	1.10	1.11	
ACRE2 (6 items)				
Percent Correct	65%	43%	61%	
Mean	3.87	2.58	3.64	.84
SD	1.46	1.41	1.53	
ACRE3 (8 items)				
Percent Correct	61%	52%	59%	
Mean	4.87	4.16	4.74	.37
SD	1.91	1.93	1.94	

ACRE1

ACRE1 contained only four items for this domain. The items concerned the identification of the four evangelists, an understanding of what happened on Pentecost, and the meaning of the Immaculate Conception and the Assumption (Figure 4.4). The performance of the students in this domain was the poorest of the domains on ACRE1.

The students performed best on the items in this domain when asked about the identity of the four evangelists. Three-fourths of those in Catholic schools knew that the identity of the four evangelists compared with 63 percent of those in parish programs. Some students named Peter, Paul and James (15% in parish programs) among the evangelists, while others included Andrew (12% in parish programs).

Less than two-thirds of the students in Catholic schools and less than half of those in parish programs recognized what happened on Pentecost and knew the meanings of the Immaculate Conception and the Assumption. The misconceptions were:

- Pentecost Sunday celebrates the baptism of Jesus (13% in Catholic schools, 25% in parish programs), Jesus dying on the cross (18% in parish programs) or Jesus returning to heaven (13% in Catholic schools, 15% in parish programs);

- The Immaculate Conception means that Mary was taken up into heaven (23% in Catholic schools, 21% in parish programs) or that Mary is a model of faith (10% in Catholic schools, 20% in parish programs);

- The Assumption signifies Jesus ascending into heaven (29% in Catholic schools, 32% in parish programs) or Jesus rising from the dead (11% in Catholic schools, 17 percent parish program).

Figure 4.4 ACRE1 - Church History

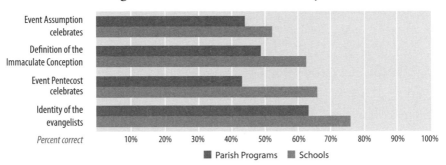

ACRE2

The poor performance on questions in the Church History domain continued for those who took ACRE2 (Figure 4.5). The one item on which the students did perform fairly well (88% in Catholic schools, 68% in parish programs) was identifying the nature of the Bible as a collection of many books written under God's inspiration, although 22 percent of those in parish programs thought that the Bible consisted only of the four Gospels. On the remaining five items, the percentage correct ranged from 47 percent to 71 percent for students from Catholic schools and from 28 percent to 46 percent for students from parish programs.

Many students continued to misidentify the meaning of two major feast days, Pentecost and the Assumption. Pentecost Sunday was selected as the time that Christians celebrate Jesus returning to heaven (13% in Catholic schools, 19% in parish programs), the baptism of Jesus (18% in parish programs) or Jesus dying on the cross (18% in parish programs). Rather than the Assumption, answered correctly by 61 percent of Catholic school students and 35 percent of students in parish programs, many students incorrectly identified the event in which Mary was taken into heaven as the Ascension (29% in Catholic schools, 43% in parish programs), the Annunciation (11% in parish programs) or the Apparition (11% in parish programs).

Sixty percent of those in Catholic schools and less than half (46%) of students in parish programs knew that the Catechumenate refers to the process of initiating people into the Church. The misconceptions of the part of some were that the Catechumenate was the process by which saints are chosen (17% in Catholic schools, 22% in parish programs), priests are formed (17% in Catholic schools, 20% in parish programs) or children are blessed (13% in parish programs).

More than sixty percent of the students in Catholic schools knew that Vatican II was the most recently held Ecumenical Council, although only 38 percent of those in parish programs selected the correct answer. The misconceptions were that the most recently held council was the United State Conference of Catholic Bishops (25% in Catholic schools, 35% in parish programs), the Council of Jerusalem (14% in parish programs), or the Council of Trent (13% in parish programs).

Figure 4.5 ACRE2 - Church History

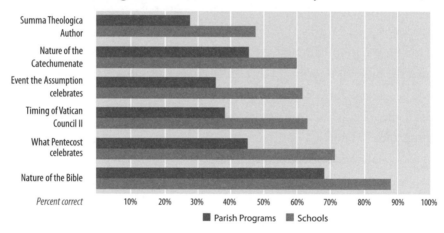

Most students who took ACRE2 had no knowledge of who wrote the *Summa Theologica*. This question had the lowest correct answer response among both groups of students. Less than half (47%) of those in Catholic schools and just 28 percent of those in parish programs identified Thomas Aquinas as the author. Others selected Theresa of Avila (22% in Catholic schools, 33% in parish programs), Catherine of Siena (18% in Catholic schools, 24% in parish programs), or Bonaventure (13% in Catholic schools, 15% in parish programs) as the author of the *Summa*. The patterns of answers provide some evidence of random guessing on the part of many students, which suggests that a majority may have never heard of the *Summa Theologica*. Perhaps, some students may have at least heard the names of Theresa of Avila and Catherine of Siena because of the relatively high number of them selecting these saints, albeit incorrectly, or perhaps they were simply guessing.

ACRE3

Despite virtually no overlap in the items in the Church History domain with the items on ACRE1 and ACRE2, the domain also proved to be the most difficult for the students who took ACRE3 (Figure 4.6). The high school students showed a slight improvement on the only item repeated from ACRE2 than did those students who took ACRE2. Sixty-six percent of Catholic school students and 57 percent of those in parish program correctly identified the purpose of the catechumenal process as initiation into the Church. Misconceptions still persisted, however, with some students identifying the purpose of the catechumenal process as training religious instructors (14% in Catholic schools, 11% in parish programs) or as priestly formation (11% in parish programs).

Most students knew that the Protestant churches were formed during the Reformation, that the reason for Vatican II was to foster renewal in the Church, and that the creed used at Sunday Mass came from the Council of Nicea. The misconceptions about these three topics were:

- Protestant churches were formed during the Apostolic Age (14% in parish programs) or the Crusades (12% in parish programs);
- Vatican II was called to clarify the meaning of papal infallibility (14% in Catholic schools, 11% in parish programs) or to solve the problem of racial discrimination (13% in parish programs);
- The creed used at Sunday Mass came from the Council of Jerusalem (17% in Catholic schools, 27% in parish programs), the Council of Constance (13% in parish programs) or the Council of Ephesus (12% in parish programs).

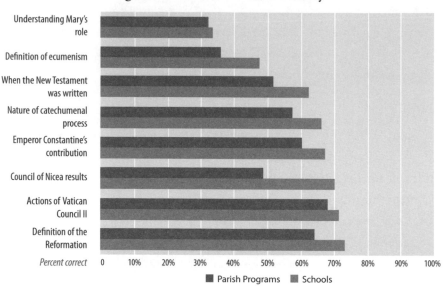

Figure 4.6 ACRE3 - Church History

Percent correct

Legend: Parish Programs | Schools

Many students who took ACRE3 did not have a clear understanding of when the New Testament was written. Sixty-two percent of those in Catholic schools and 57 percent in parish programs correctly answered that the formation of the New Testament occurred during the Apostolic Age. On the other hand, some thought that the New Testament was written during the Reformation (17% in Catholic schools, 22% in parish programs), the Age of Enlightenment (12% in Catholic schools, 15% in parish programs), or before the time of Christ (12% in parish programs).

Most students also didn't understand the meaning of the term "ecumenism." Less than half recognized that ecumenism is the name of the movement toward unity among Christians and Christian churches. A substantial number incorrectly identified ecumenism with conversion (28% in Catholic schools, 29% in parish programs), redemption (15% in Catholic schools, 20% in parish programs), or preaching (15% in parish programs).

The question in the domain that gave the students the most trouble concerned Catholic teaching about Mary. Some of the trouble may have been due to the way the item was presented. Students were asked to identify a statement about Mary that was contrary to Catholic teaching. Only one-third of the students correctly identified that a statement contrary to Catholic teaching was that Mary overcame the burden of original sin when she agreed to become the Mother of God. Generally, questions that request a wrong answer or an exception are more difficult for students. On the other hand, the students still should have been able to eliminate the statements about Mary that were in accord with Catholic teaching. The following are the tenets of Catholic teaching about Mary that many students incorrectly identified as contrary to Catholic teaching:

- Mary is one of the poor and humble of the world who awaits the fulfillment of God's promise (31% in Catholic schools, 27% in parish programs);

- Mary is the new Eve and the mother of all humankind (21% in Catholic schools, 24% in parish programs);

- Mary is the model of faith and fidelity for Christians and the Church (15% in Catholic schools, 17% in parish programs).

Summary

Overall, the performance of the students on this domain at all levels was the poorest of all the domains. Only one area of particular strength was noted and that concerned a good understanding of nature of the Bible by students who took ACRE2.

Areas of weakness in this domain include a lack of understanding of the significance of Pentecost Sunday (ACRE1, ACRE2), the meaning of major feast days of the Immaculate Conception (ACRE1) and the Assumption (ACRE1, ACRE2), the identity of the Evangelists (ACRE1), the meaning and significance of the term Catechumenate (ACRE2, ACRE3)), when Vatican II was held (ACRE2), when the New Testament was written (ACRE3), the meaning of the term ecumenism (ACRE3), the identity of the author of the *Summa Theologica* (ACRE2), and a proper understanding of Mary's role in the Church ACRE3).

Domain 7
Prayer and Religious Practice

The items on Domain 7 concern the students' understanding of prayer and traditional devotional practices.

Key Objective

Recognize and learn how to engage in Catholic forms of personal prayer and ways of deepening one's spiritual life

Key Concepts

Traditional Catholic prayers; Sacramentals; Rosary, Stations of the Cross, holy water; devotional practices rooted in different cultures; purpose and forms of prayer; Precepts of the Church; Spirituality

Table 4.3 presents the summary statistics for the seventh domain of faith knowledge: Prayer and Religious Practices. On average, Catholic school students answered 74 percent of the items correctly and students from parish religious education programs answered 63 percent correctly. A large difference (effect size = .77) occurs between the performance of students in Catholic schools and those in parish programs on ACRE1. The difference between the performance of students in Catholic schools and those in parish programs is in the medium range for ACRE2 (.37) and in the small range for ACRE3 (.30).

Table 4.3 ACRE Results: 2004-2005
Domain 7: Prayer/Religious Practices

	Catholics in Catholic School	Catholics in Parish Programs	Total	Effect Size
ACRE1 (6 items)				
Percent Correct	69%	52%	66%	
Mean	4.13	3.12	3.94	.77
SD	1.25	1.31	1.32	
ACRE2 (5 items)				
Percent Correct	76%	68%	74%	
Mean	3.79	3.38	3.71	.37
SD	1.08	1.22	1.12	

Table 4.3 continued

	Catholics in Catholic School	Catholics in Parish Programs	Total	Effect Size
ACRE3 (8 items)				
Percent Correct	76%	69%	74%	
Mean	6.07	5.55	5.94	.30
SD	1.66	1.74	1.72	

ACRE1

The average score on the Prayer/Religious Practice domain was 66 percent correct, which made this domain the third worse in overall performance for the students who took ACRE1 (Table 4.3).

With some notable exceptions, the students showed adequate to good understanding of the nature of the Stations of the Cross, the importance and content of the Our Father, and the Rosary as a devotion to Mary (Figure 4.7). The misconceptions were that, rather than the Our Father, Jesus taught his disciples to pray when he taught them the Apostles' Creed (11% in Catholic schools, 16% in parish programs), and confusion on the wording of the Our Father as "we ask God to forgive us as we forgive our own sins" (21% in Catholic schools, 35% in parish programs).

Figure 4.7 ACRE1 - Prayer/Religious Practice

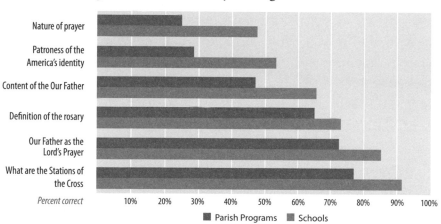

The students also had difficulty with identifying intercession/petition as the type of prayer offered for the needs of the community and the world (47% in Catholic schools, 25% in parish programs). Incorrect choices included blessing (35% in Catholic schools, 57% in parish programs) or thanksgiving (12% in Catholic schools, 11% in parish programs).

Just over half of the Catholic school students and only 29 percent of those in parish programs were aware that Our Lady of Guadalupe is the patroness of the Americas. When asked to identify the patroness of the Americas, many students instead incorrectly selected Elizabeth, the mother of John the Baptist (15% in Catholic schools, 29% in parish programs), Anne, the mother of Mary (14% in Catholic schools, 24% in parish programs), or Our Lady of Lourdes (18% in Catholic schools, 19% in parish programs).

ACRE2

The overall performance of the 8th and 9th grade students on the Prayer/Religious Practice domain of ACRE2 was better than that of the younger students who took ACRE1 (Table 4.3). The items on ACRE2, however, to a great extent were more intuitive, and thus perhaps easier, than those on ACRE1. For example, on ACRE1 students were asked to identify the type of prayer that is offered for the needs of the community and the world. This turned out to be a difficult item for the students with only 43 percent answering correctly that the type was intercessory prayer or petition. On ACRE2, students were asked to indicate which of four statements about prayer would be rejected by the Church. Eighty-nine percent of the students picked the obvious wrong response that the prayers of sinners go unanswered by God.

The students who took ACRE2 understood that God answers prayers of sinners as well as the just, that cultural differences occur in the expression of faith, and that spirituality is a term used to identify our growing and loving relationship with God (Figure 4.8).

Most students recognized that an obligation that Catholics have once a year is to receive Holy Communion during the Easter Season. A few students failed to recognize that, however, selecting instead that the obligation was to support the Church (14% in Catholic schools, 19% in parish programs).

Figure 4.8 ACRE2 - Prayer/Religious Practice

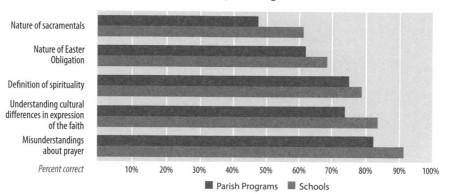

The one item on which both students from Catholic schools and those from parish programs experienced some difficulty concerned their understanding of the nature of a sacramental. Those who answered incorrectly indicated that sacramentals are special prayers the priests says when administering the sacraments (19% in Catholic schools, 27% in parish programs) or that sacramentals give the grace of the Holy Spirit in the same way that as the celebration of the sacraments (18% in Catholic schools, 22% in parish programs).

ACRE3

The average performance of students on the Prayer/Religious Practice in ACRE3 is equal to the average performance of those who took ACRE2 (Table 4.3). As in ACRE2, the case could be made that the items in this domain for ACRE3 are quite intuitive, therefore easier for students (Figure 4.9). For example, the item about Our Lady of Guadalupe on ACRE3 prompts students that the event occurred in Mexico, whereas a corresponding item on ACRE1 asks the students to identify the patroness of the Americas, without providing additional clues. Likewise, the question about a sacramental on ACRE3 asks about its general purpose, whereas a corresponding item on ACRE2 explores the nature of a sacramental, which requires a student to know more specific information about a sacramental, thus increasing the difficulty of the item.

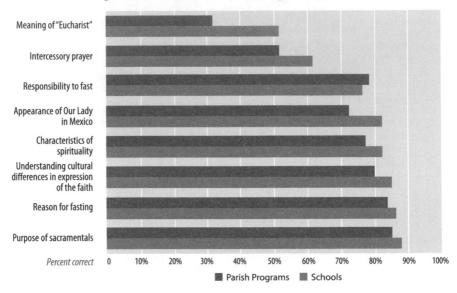

Figure 4.9 ACRE3 - Prayer/Religious Practice

The items on which many students had difficulty concerned the definition of intercessory prayer and the understanding that Eucharist denotes "thanksgiving." Those who answered these items incorrectly were more likely to say that the type of prayer in which people pray on behalf of others is called adoration (26% in Catholic schools, 31% in parish programs) and/or that the words "blessing" (29% in Catholic schools, 43% in parish programs) or "benediction" (15% in Catholic schools, 20% in parish programs), rather than "Eucharist," means thanksgiving.

Summary

The students generally understood the nature of the Stations of the Cross (ACRE1), the importance of the Lord's Prayer (ACRE1), the significance of the Rosary as a devotion to Mary (ACRE1), the definition and characteristics of spirituality (ACRE2, ACRE3), the necessity of cultural differences in the expression of the faith (ACRE2), and the reasons for fasting (ACRE3).

The students misunderstood the types of prayer (ACRE1, ACRE3) and the meaning of Eucharist (ACRE3). Older students recognized Mexico as the place where Our Lady of Guadalupe appeared (ACRE3); however, younger students failed to recognize the identity of the Patroness of the Americas (ACRE1). High school students generally understood the nature of sacramentals (ACRE3); however, middle school students did not (ACRE2).

Domain 8
Catholic Faith Literacy

The items in Domain 8 deal with definition of Catholic religious terms and knowledge of doctrinal matters.

Key Objective
Be literate in the use of Catholic religious terminology

Key Concepts
A large number of concepts related to each of the seven previous domains; Christian Hope: eschatology, final judgment, heaven, hell, purgatory

Table 4.4 presents the summary statistics for the domain of faith knowledge: Catholic Faith Literacy. On average, Catholic school students answered 72 percent of the items correctly and students from parish religious education programs answered 59 percent correctly. A large difference (effect size = .77) once again is evident between the performance of students in Catholic schools and those in parish programs on ACRE2. The difference between the performance of students in Catholic schools and those in parish programs is in the medium range for ACRE1 (.53) and ACRE3 (.54).

Table 4.4 ACRE Results: 2004-2005
Domain 8: Catholic Faith Literacy

	Catholics in Catholic School	Catholics in Parish Programs	Total	Effect Size
ACRE1 (7 items)				
Percent Correct	78%	68%	76%	
Mean	5.49	4.78	5.34	.53
SD	1.29	1.41	1.35	
ACRE2 (7 items)				
Percent Correct	69%	53%	66%	
Mean	4.85	3.70	4.65	.77
SD	1.42	1.53	1.50	
ACRE3 (6 items)				
Percent Correct	69%	56%	67%	
Mean	4.16	3.34	4.04	.54
SD	1.47	1.48	1.51	

ACRE1

The students who took ACRE1 showed good understanding of saints, Jesus, heaven, and the pope (Figure 4.10). Most (77% in Catholic schools; 66% in parish programs) also understood the meaning of the Resurrection; however, some (18% in Catholic schools, 22% in parish programs) misidentified the Resurrection as signifying Jesus' ascension into heaven.

Just over half of those in Catholic schools and about four in ten of those in parish programs correctly recognized the role of the Creed in the Mass and the meaning of covenant in the Old Testament. Many identified the Lord's Prayer (34% in Catholic schools, 47% in parish programs) or the Glory to the Father (13% in parish programs) as the affirmation of our beliefs as Catholics that occurs during the Mass. The covenant of the Old Testament was misidentified as prophecy (26% in Catholic schools, 30% in parish programs), prayer (11% in Catholic schools, 17% in parish programs) or community (13% in parish programs).

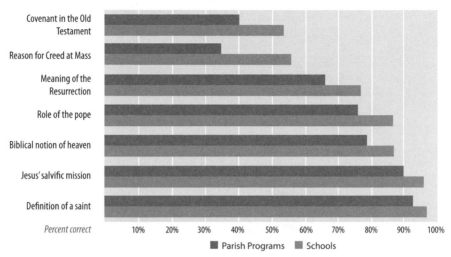

Figure 4.10 ACRE1 - Catholic Faith Literacy

ACRE2

The vast majority of the students who took ACRE2 understood the nature of abortion and some reasons for belonging to a parish (Figure 4.11). Those in Catholic schools more than those in parish programs knew the definition of a martyr and the meaning of the Incarnation. Students in both Catholic schools and parish programs, however, had trouble with recognizing the importance of the Resurrection and the definitions of ecumenism and the Magisterium. Some common misconceptions on the items in this domain were:

- Rather than martyrs, saints who died for their faith are called apostles (23% in parish programs) or disciples (19% in parish programs);

- Rather than the Incarnation, the mystery by which the Son of God became man is called the Ascension (12% in Catholic schools, 21% in parish programs) or the Resurrection (17% in parish programs);

- Rather than the Magisterium, the Church's office that teaches on faith and morals is called the parish council (40% in Catholic schools, 45% in parish programs), Holy Orders (14% in Catholic schools, 22% in parish programs) or the Hierarchy (10% in Catholic schools, 11% in parish programs);

- Rather than the Resurrection, the event in Jesus' life that confirms all that he taught about himself and the kingdom of God is the Transfiguration (21% in Catholic schools, 18% in parish programs), Crucifixion (15% in Catholic schools, 23% in parish programs), or Incarnation (12% in parish programs);

- Rather than ecumenism, the movement toward unity among Christians and Christian churches is called conversion (22% in Catholic schools, 24% in parish programs), preaching (20% in Catholic schools, 28% in parish programs) or redemption (14% in Catholic schools, 20% in parish programs).

Figure 4.11 ACRE2 - Catholic Faith Literacy

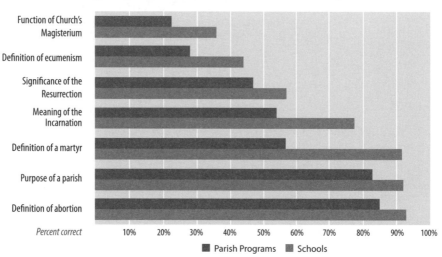

ACRE3

Both those in schools and in parish programs understood the purpose of the homily at Mass (Figure 4.12). Many students, but more in Catholic schools than those in parish programs, knew the definitions of grace, Incarnation, and virtue. Some in parish programs confused a sacramental with grace (18% in parish programs) and the Ascension (16% in parish programs) and Resurrection (14% in parish programs) with the Incarnation. Finally, some students failed to draw the proper distinction in defining a virtue when they selected the response that a virtue is doing a good deed (23% in Catholic schools, 29% in parish programs) instead of a being a habit or pattern of doing good.

Neither students in Catholic schools nor those in parish program performed adequately in knowing that the Gospels writers were called evangelists (59% in Catholic schools, 29% in parish programs). When asked what the Gospel writers were called, many students incorrectly selected the apostles (20% in Catholic schools, 31% in parish programs), the disciples (11% in Catholic schools, 22% in parish programs) or the prophets (10% in Catholic schools, 18% in parish programs).

Furthermore, half of those in Catholic schools and slightly less than half of those in parish programs understood the condition necessary for the Church to grant an annulment to a marriage. Most students who answered the item incorrectly (29% in Catholic schools, 31% in parish programs) thought that a condition for an annulment is that the marriage has broken down with no possibility to restore it. Others incorrectly thought that a condition would be that one of members had been unfaithful (13% in Catholic schools, 18% in parish programs) or that the couple no longer loves one another (12% in parish programs).

Figure 4.12 ACRE3 - Catholic Faith Literacy

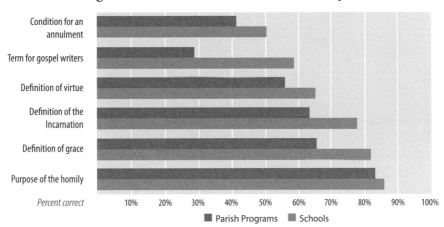

Summary

With regard to literacy, the students had a good understanding of Jesus' salvific mission (ACRE1), the biblical notion of heaven (ACRE1), saints (ACRE1), the role of the pope (ACRE1), the purpose of a parish (ACRE2), the definition of abortion (ACRE2), the purpose of the homily at Mass (ACRE3), the meaning of the Incarnation (ACRE3), and the definition of grace (ACRE3).

The students had trouble with understanding the significance of the covenant in the Old Testament (ACRE1), the reason for the Creed at Mass (ACRE1), the meaning and significance of the Resurrection (ACRE1, ACRE2), the role of the Church's Magisterium (ACRE2), the definition of ecumenism (ACRE2), the meaning of the Incarnation (ACRE2), the definition of a martyr (ACRE2), the term identifying the Gospel writers (ACRE3), and the conditions for an annulment of a marriage (ACRE3).

Chapter 5
Beliefs, Attitudes, Practices and Perceptions

Introduction

C hapter 5 presents the responses of the Catholic students in Catholic schools and those in parish programs to the items in Part 2 of ACRE that measure beliefs, attitudes, practices and perceptions. The first section of the chapter contains an analysis of the average responses to the items that constitute seven subscales: Relationship with Jesus, Images of God, Catholic Identity, Morality, Family Relationships/Communication, Perceptions of the Religion Program/Parish, and Vocations. The second section contains comparisons of the average performance on the subscales according to the different levels of ACRE for students from Catholic schools and those from parish programs. The third section presents a summary of the perceptions of students who attended Catholic schools and those from other schools about the relative seriousness of various problems that occur in their schools.

The tables in this chapter contain the mean (average) scale scores and the percent agreement to the items in Part 2. The students responded to each item using a 4-step Likert scale (4 = Strongly Agree, 3 = Agree, 2 = Disagree and 1 = Strongly Disagree). As a result, the average score for each item ranges between 4.00 and 1.00, with a higher average indicating greater agreement. The percentages of Strongly Agree responses and those for Total Agreement, which is the sum of the Strongly Agree and Agree responses, are both included in the tables. Additional analyses and tables are presented for those items where differences between the mean scores of Catholic students in Catholic schools and those in parish programs have effect sizes of .25 or greater. These are considered meaningful differences between the two groups of students. The figures in the chapter display in graphical form the percentage of total agreement to the items within each subscale for each level of ACRE.

Section 1: Performance on the Seven Subscales

Relationship with Jesus

Table 5.1 shows the mean scale scores and percent agreement to the items on the Relationship with Jesus subscale. For all three levels of ACRE, the Catholic students in both school and parish programs showed strong agreement with the quality and strength of their relationships with Jesus (see Figure 5.1). Over 90 percent viewed Jesus as their Savior and friend. Between 80 percent (ACRE3) and 95 percent (ACRE1) felt that Jesus really understands them and that their relationship with Jesus really helps them. Over 90 percent of the students responded that they believed that Jesus cured the blind and raised the dead, perhaps an indication that they believed in Jesus' miracles and by extension, His divinity.

Table 5.1 Mean Scale Scores and Percent Agreement to Relationship with Jesus Subscale

	Mean Scores			Strongly Agree / Total Agreement[1]		
Relationship with Jesus	ACRE1	ACRE2	ACRE3	ACRE1	ACRE2	ACRE3
I look upon Jesus as my Savior and friend	3.78	3.69	3.51	79/99	72/98	59/94
I believe that Jesus cured the blind and raised the dead	3.68	3.58	3.35	73/95	64/94	49/89
I feel Jesus really understands me	3.63	3.33	3.06	69/95	45/89	30/80
Jesus' relationship with me really helps me	3.54	3.29	3.06	60/95	41/90	30/80

---

[1] The first number is the percentage of students who strongly agree with the statement. The second number is the percentage of students who strongly agree or agree with the statement. This same format is followed in the tables throughout this chapter.

The only item on ACRE 1 on which Catholic school students scored markedly higher than students from parish programs was in their belief that Jesus cured the blind and raised the dead (see Table 5.2). Otherwise, no meaningful differences between Catholic school students and parish student were evident on the other items for those who took ACRE1 and ACRE 2.

On the other hand, high school students in parish programs who took ACRE3 showed more favorable attitudes toward feeling that Jesus understood them and that their relationship with Jesus helped them than did students in Catholic high schools (see Table 5.2). While the total agreement of both groups of students was similar, a higher percentage of students in parish programs (41% and 39%) than students in Catholic high schools (29% to both items) strongly agreed with these two items.

Table 5.2 Meaningful Differences on the Relationship with Jesus Subscale

	Mean Scores			Strongly Agree / Total Agreement	
Relationship with Jesus	School	Parish Program	Effect Size[2]	School	Parish Program
ACRE1					
I believe that Jesus cured the blind and raised the dead	3.71	3.50	.34	76/96	61/91
ACRE3					
I feel Jesus really understands me	3.05	3.26	−.28	29/80	41/87
Jesus' relationship with me really helps me	3.05	3.27	−.28	29/80	39/90

The findings concerning the students' relationship with Jesus are similar to those obtained from the analysis of the 1994-1995 data for the previous version of ACRE (Convey & Thompson, 1999). In addition, the findings from the 1994-1995 administration and earlier results from the predecessor of ACRE (Thompson, 1982) have shown that how students relate to Jesus is

---

[2] Items with effect sizes of .25 or greater (medium to large effects) are included.

important to their overall performance on religious knowledge and their acceptance of other Catholic practices. The very positive results concerning students' stated relationships with Jesus are encouraging since a purpose of a Catholic education is to proclaim Jesus Christ and his saving message. Pope Benedict XVI in his address to Catholic educators at The Catholic University of America on April 17, 2008 reminded them that "Education is integral to the mission of the Church to proclaim the Good News. First and foremost every Catholic educational institution is a place to encounter the living God, who in Jesus Christ reveals his transforming love and truth."

Figure 5.1 Percent Agreement on Items Pertaining to Students' Relationship with Jesus

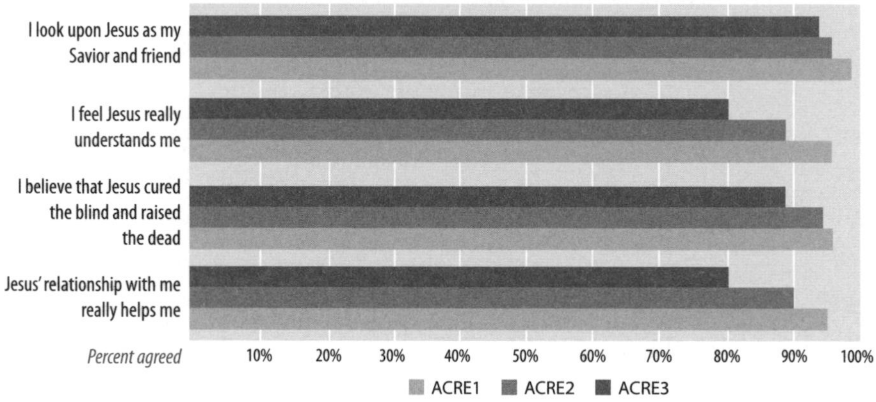

Images of God

Table 5.3 presents the mean scale scores and percent agreement to the items on the Images of God subscale. Students at all levels of ACRE had very strong beliefs in God's love for them even when they sin and high confidence that God does listen to their prayers (Figure 5.2). The students also generally agreed that one way that God speaks to them is through the Bible. A clear decrease is evident, however, in the students' favorable images of God as the assessment progresses from younger students to older students (ACRE1 to ACRE3). Older students are more likely than younger students to think of God as a strict judge and less likely to agree that God still loves them when they sin, that God listens to them when they pray, and that God speaks to them through the Bible.

Table 5.3 Mean Scale Scores and
Percent Agreement to Images of God Subscale

	Mean Scores			Strongly Agree / Total Agreement		
Images of God	ACRE1	ACRE2	ACRE3	ACRE1	ACRE2	ACRE3
Even when I sin, God still loves me	3.80	3.69	3.51	81/99	72/98	58/96
When I pray, God really does listen to me	3.54	3.42	3.31	62/95	52/93	46/89
I would like to learn how to get closer to God	n/a	n/a	3.20	n/a	n/a	38/86
One way that God speaks to me is through the Bible	3.18	3.02	2.80	37/83	27/79	19/68
My friends and I talk about God	2.58	2.41	2.49	11/57	6/47	11/51
I think of God as a strict judge	1.56	1.90	2.08	3/11	4/18	5/23

Meaningful differences between Catholic school students and students from parish programs occur on one item on ACRE1 and three items on ACRE3 (see Table 5.4). No meaningful differences between the groups, however, are present on ACRE2. On ACRE1 Catholic school students showed higher agreement than did students from parish religious education programs to talking to their friends about God (effect size = .28). Such a finding might be anticipated in that many friends of students in a Catholic school were likely to be in the same Catholic school where conversations about God presumably occur on a regular basis in a school setting, but perhaps less frequently in informal conversations among friends as evidence by the somewhat lower levels of agreement shown in Table 5.4 (59% for Catholic school students and 46% for parish religious education students).

Table 5.4 Meaningful Differences on the Images of God Subscale

	Average			Strongly Agree / Total Agreement	
Images of God	School	Parish Program	Effect Size	School	Parish Program
ACRE1					
My friends and I talk about God	2.61	2.39	.28	11/59	8/46
ACRE3					
I would like to learn how to get closer to God	3.19	3.38	–.26	36/86	48/92
One way that God speaks to me is through the Bible	2.79	3.10	–.38	18/67	31/83
I think of God as a judge	2.07	2.27	.26	5/23	10/33

For ACRE3, the strength of students' beliefs and attitudes was higher for students from parish programs than for Catholic school students on two items. The 11th and 12th graders still participating in parish religious education programs were more likely than the students in Catholic high schools to agree that God speaks to them through the Bible. In addition, the students from parish programs were more likely to agree that they would like to get closer to God. In the previous version of ACRE (Convey & Thompson, 1999), students at all levels of ACRE showed strong agreement with a desire to learn how to get closer to God. In the current version the item about learning to get closer to God appeared only on ACRE3; however, students strongly subscribed to it (over 85 percent of all students agreed with the sentiment) as other students had in the previous version. One of the purposes of catechesis and, indeed, one of its challenges is to help students realize this desire for greater closeness to God.

As was the case in previous versions of ACRE (Convey & Thompson, 1999), only a small percentage of students think of God as a strict judge, although the percentage of older students who do so is higher than the percentages of younger students. The only meaningful difference in the responses to this item for students from Catholic schools and parish programs occurs on

ACRE3, with those from parish programs being more likely to think about God as a strict judge. Even so, only about a third of the students in parish programs agreed that they thought about God in this way.

Figure 5.2 Percent Agreement on Images of God

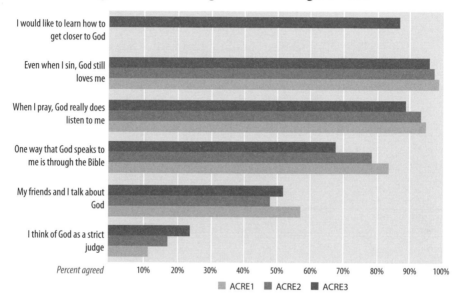

Catholic Identity

Table 5.5 presents the mean scale scores and percent agreement to the items on the Catholic Identity subscale. Of the four items on the subscale, two are measuring attitudes (importance of being a Catholic and importance of praying the rosary) and two are measuring practices (attending Mass and participating in the sacrament of Penance).

The vast majority of students, over 90 percent of those who took ACRE1 and ACRE2 and 85 percent of those who took ACRE3, agreed that being a Catholic was important for them (see Figure 5.3). Student attitudes toward the devotional practice of the importance of praying the rosary, however, were lower. Approximately, eight in ten students who took ACRE1 agreed that praying the rosary was important for them; however, only six in ten who took ACRE2 and four in ten who took ACRE3 thought so. Students in

Catholic high schools and parish programs had similar attitudes toward the importance of being a Catholic and the importance of praying the rosary on ACRE1 and ACRE2, but students in parish programs had higher levels of agreement than did Catholic high school students toward these sentiments on ACRE3 (see Table 5.6).

Table 5.5 Mean Scale Scores and Percent Agreement to Catholic Identity Subscale

	Mean Scores			Strongly Agree / Total Agreement		
Catholic Identity	**ACRE1**	**ACRE2**	**ACRE3**	**ACRE1**	**ACRE2**	**ACRE3**
Being a Catholic is important to me	3.58	3.45	3.22	58/92	53/94	42/85
I participate in the sacrament of Penance	3.40	3.16	2.73	47/91	34/85	18/65
I attend Saturday evening / Sunday Mass	3.18	3.14	2.93	38/83	41/78	37/67
Praying the rosary is important to me	3.09	2.70	2.34	26/84	11/64	8/39

The pattern of responses to the practices of attending Mass on a regular basis and participating in the sacrament of Penance clearly shows that older students valued these practices that are important for Catholics less than did younger students. For example, two-thirds of the high school students who took ACRE3 agreed that they attend Mass on Saturday evenings or Sundays, compared with more than three-fourths of those who took ACRE2 and more than 80 percent of those who took ACRE1. It should be noted, however, that the frequency of attending Mass on weekends cannot be inferred from this item since the students were simply asked to state their agreement as to whether they attend Mass on weekends, not how often[3]. In comparison, 52

---

[3] In the National Survey of Youth and Religion, 2002-3 (Christian Smith, *Soul Searching*, Oxford University Press, 2005) 55 percent of Catholic adolescents age 13-17 reported attending religious services once a week or more. A composite of results from surveys conducted by the Center for Research in the Apostolate show that approximately 35 percent of Catholic adults report attending Mass regularly on weekends.

percent of students who took ACRE in 1994-1995 indicated they attended Mass on weekends.

The pattern of older students valuing traditional religious practice less than younger students also was observed for participation in the sacrament of Penance. Older students reported lower agreement than did younger students about receiving the sacrament of Reconciliation. Except for the higher agreement about participation in the sacrament of Penance by Catholic school students on ACRE2 (see Table 5.6), no differences occurred in the agreement of students from Catholic schools and parish programs to attending mass and going to confession on ACRE1 and ACRE2. On ACRE3, however, once again the high school students from parish programs showed higher levels of agreement on the frequency of attending Mass and receiving the sacrament of Penance than did the students from Catholic high schools (see Table 5.6).

Table 5.6 Meaningful Differences on the Catholic Identity Subscale

	Average			Strongly Agree / Total Agreement	
Catholic Identity	School	Parish Program	Effect Size	School	Parish Program
ACRE2					
I participate in the sacrament of Penance	3.18	3.00	.25	34/87	28/77
ACRE3					
Being a Catholic is important to me	3.21	3.46	−.31	40/89	55/93
I participate in the sacrament of Penance	2.72	2.99	−.32	17/64	26/78
I attend Saturday evening / Sunday Mass	2.91	3.39	−.48	36/66	48/92
Praying the rosary is important to me	2.33	2.58	−.32	7/49	10/55

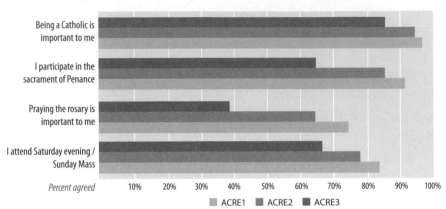

Figure 5.3 Percent Agreement on Catholic Identity

Morality

Table 5.7 presents the mean scale scores and percent agreement to the items on the Morality subscale. The items assessing moral judgment concerned personal moral practices, cheating, drugs and alcohol and sexual morality (see Figure 5.4). In terms of personal moral practices, about eight in ten students indicated that they take time to think about whether their actions are right or wrong. The majority of students also agreed that they discuss moral issues with their friends; however, the pattern of responses indicates that younger students do this more frequently than older students[4]. There were no differences, however, in the level of agreement of those in Catholic schools and those in parish programs. The students also showed strong affirmation to personally being responsible for making the world a better place, with those who took ACRE3 (72%) showing a slightly higher level of agreement than did those who took ACRE2 (63%).

---

[4]The item for ACRE3 (My friends and I talk about moral issues) was slightly different than the item for ACRE1 and ACRE2 (My friends and I talk about things that are right and wrong).

Table 5.7 Mean Scale Scores and Percent Agreement to Morality Subscale

	Mean Scores			Strongly Agree / Total Agreement		
Morality	ACRE1	ACRE2	ACRE3	ACRE1	ACRE2	ACRE3
It is OK for people my age to drink alcohol at a party	n/a	1.56	2.39	n/a	3/11	11/47
I think abortion is wrong under any condition	n/a	3.23	3.04	n/a	56.76	47/67
It is important to me to wait until marriage before having sexual intercourse	n/a	3.09	2.67	n/a	41/75	26.55
It is alright for a couple to live together before getting married	n/a	2.91	2.91	n/a	25/74	23/75
I take time to think about whether my actions are right or wrong	2.99	2.92	3.03	21/81	17/78	21/84
My friends and I talk about things that are right or wrong	2.88	2.99	n/a	21/73	25/79	n/a
My friends and I talk about moral issues	n/a	n/a	2.81	n/a	n/a	21/68
It is OK to copy a friend's homework if you do not have time to get yours done	1.41	1.96	2.29	1/5	3/10	7/37
It is all right to try drugs	1.10	1.31	1.77	1/2	1/6	4/20
I am personally responsible for making the world a better place	n/a	2.73	2.88	n/a	17/63	21/72

With regard to cheating and the use of drugs, older students were more accepting of copying homework and trying drugs than younger students; however, in all cases the percentages of agreement were low. Those in Catholic high schools showed more tolerance for drug use than did those in parish programs (see Table 5.8), although, once again, the percentage in Catholic high schools who agreed that it's all right to try drugs was low (20%).

The use of alcohol among high school students is a national problem. Therefore, it is not surprising that the responses to the item about the use of alcohol on ACRE2 and ACRE3 indicated that older high school students were more accepting of drinking alcohol at parties than were younger students.

Almost 1 in 2 students who took ACRE3 indicated it was all right for people their age to drink alcohol at a party, compared with about 1 in 10 students on ACRE2.

Items concerning sexual morality were on ACRE2 and ACRE3, but not on ACRE1. Most students agreed that abortion is wrong under any condition (76% ACRE2; 67% ACRE3) and that it is important to wait until marriage before having sexual intercourse (75% ACRE2; 55% ACRE3). On the other hand, over seven in ten students deviated from church teaching regarding the morality of living together before getting married. Those who took ACRE3 (75%) showed about the same level of agreement in their responses as those who took ACRE2 (74%) for the acceptability of couples living together before getting married, although the students who took ACRE2 (75%) were more in agreement than those who took ACRE3 (55%) that it was important to wait until marriage before having sexual intercourse. On ACRE3 the high school students in parish programs more than the Catholic students in Catholic high schools held attitudes about sexual mores that were closer to the teachings of the Church (see Table 5.8).

Table 5.8 Meaningful Differences on the Morality Subscale

	Average			Strongly Agree / Total Agreement	
Morality	School	Parish Program	Effect Size	School	Parish Program
ACRE3					
It is important to me to wait until marriage before having sexual intercourse	2.66	3.03	–.38	24/54	38/71
It is all right for a couple to live together before getting married	2.92	2.66	–.31	24/75	17/62
It is all right to try drugs	1.79	1.51	–.33	4/20	2/11

Figure 5.4 Percent Agreement about Moral Issues

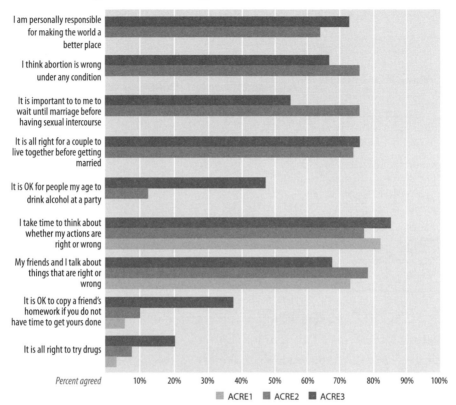

Family Relationships/Communication

Earlier research on ACRE (Convey & Thompson, 1999) and its predecessor (Thompson, 1982) showed the importance of the family in influencing the religious practices of their children. In the study using the 1994-1995 data from ACRE (Convey & Thompson, 1999), a student's reported relationship with her or his family was the most important predictor of religious practice for fifth graders and a significant predictor of religious practice for 11th and 12th graders. The Family Relationships/Communication subscale in this current study contains three of the items that were important components of the family relationship construct used in the 1994-1995 study: the importance of family dinners, the family praying together, and students talking to their parents about serious issues.

Table 5.9 Mean Scale Scores and Percent Agreement
on Family Relationships/Communication Subscale

	Mean Scores			Strongly Agree / Total Agreement		
Family Relationships / Communication	ACRE1	ACRE2	ACRE3	ACRE1	ACRE2	ACRE3
If I thought a friend were getting addicted to drugs or alcohol, I would talk to an adult I trust	n/a	3.25	3.05	n/a	47/82	35/76
Gathering together for the family meal, whenever possible, is important to my family	3.40	3.18	3.05	52/89	39/82	34/77
I talk about the most serious issues with one or both of my parents	3.32	2.81	2.74	48/87	24/67	22/62
My family prays together at home	2.86	2.65	2.42	26/67	17/58	13/46

Table 5.9 presents the mean scale scores and percent agreement to the items on the Family Relationships/Communication subscale. Students on all levels of ACRE showed high agreement to the importance of the family gathering together for meals whenever possible (see Figure 5.5). In addition, most students agreed that they talked to their parents about serious issues. Somewhat less agreement was evident in the item that asked about the practice of the family praying together at home. Slightly less than 70 percent of those who took ACRE1, slightly less than 60 percent of those who took ACRE2, and slightly less than 50 percent of those who took ACRE3 indicated that their families prayed together at home[5]. The level of agreement to all three items diminished from ACRE1 to ACRE3.

Students on ACRE2 and ACRE3 were asked about talking to someone if they thought a friend was getting addicted to drugs or alcohol. Over 80 percent of the 8th and 9th graders and 77 percent of the 11th and 12th graders agreed

---

[5] In the National Survey of Youth and Religion, 2002-3 (Smith, 2005), 67 percent of Catholic adolescents age 13-17 reported that the family prays before or after dinner.

that they would talk to an adult that they trusted if they thought a friend were getting addicted to drugs or alcohol.

No meaningful differences in the agreement of students in Catholic schools and those in parish programs were evident on responses to the items on the Family Relationships/Communication subscale.

Figure 5.5 Percent Agreement on Family Relationships/Communication Items

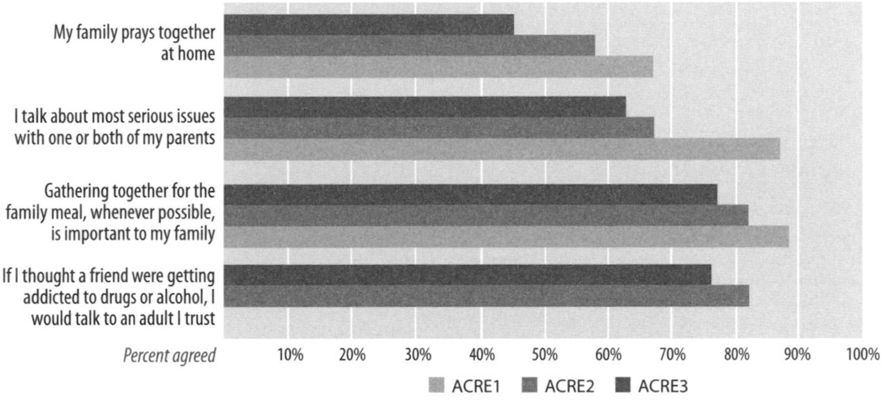

Perceptions of the Religion Program/Parish[6]

Table 5.10 presents the mean scale scores and percent agreement to the items on the Religion Program and Parish subscales. All in all, the students gave a very positive report about the environment of their religious education programs, whether in Catholic schools or in parishes (Figure 5.6). The vast majority of students across all levels of ACRE were glad to be in their school or parish program. Over 80 percent indicated that their teachers have had a positive influence on how they think and live and that their religion programs encourage volunteer work. Over 70 percent indicated that the students in their programs really care about each other, although the percentage of students who strongly agreed with that was rather low (18% to 20%). No meaningful

---

[6] The two subscales, Religion Program and Parish, were combined for the purpose of this presentation.

differences existed between the responses of students in Catholic schools and those in parish programs to items referring to their respective religion programs.

Table 5.10 Mean Scale Scores and Percent Agreement to Religion Program and Parish Subscales

Religion Program / Parish	Mean Scores			Strongly Agree / Total Agreement		
	ACRE1	ACRE2	ACRE3	ACRE1	ACRE2	ACRE3
I am glad to be in this school / parish religion program	3.46	3.15	3.08	55/93	34/85	30/83
Some of my religion teachers have been a positive influence on how I think and live	3.25	3.06	3.01	42/87	29/81	26/80
Our religion program encourages us to do volunteer work	3.01	3.04	3.23	23/81	2/80	39/86
Students here really care about each other	2.95	2.86	2.86	20/77	17/74	18/73
I belong to an excellent parish	3.62	3.30	3.00	6.95	44/89	30/77
People in my parish care about helping others	3.59	3.34	3.16	63/97	42/94	31/88
I am glad to be in this school/ parish religion program	3.46	3.15	3.08	55/93	34/85	30/83

All students also showed strong agreement to the excellence of their parish and the care that people in their parishes have for helping others. Younger students reported higher levels of agreement that they belonged to an excellent parish than did older students (ACRE1 95%; ACRE2 89%; ACRE3 77%). The students from parish programs who took ACRE3 had more favorable responses toward the excellence of their parish and their perceptions that people in the parish care about helping others than were the students from Catholic high schools (see Table 5.11). No meaningful differences toward their parishes for Catholic school students and those in parish religious education programs were evident on ACRE1 and ACRE2.

Table 5.11 Meaningful Differences on the Parish Subscale

Religion Program / Parish	Average			Strongly Agree / Total Agreement	
	School	Parish Program	Effect Size	School	Parish Program
ACRE3					
I belong to an excellent parish	2.99	3.32	–.40	29/76	46/90
People in my parish care about helping others	3.15	3.36	–.30	31/87	44/93

Figure 5.6 Percent Agreement on Perceptions of Religion Program/Parish

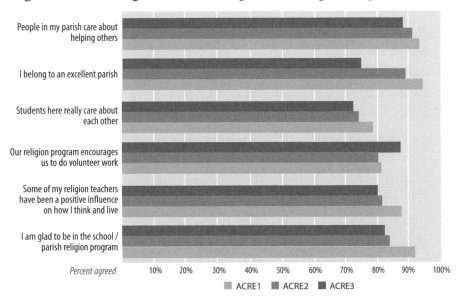

Vocations

Table 5.12 presents the mean scale scores and percent agreement to the single item dealing with vocations. With regard to thinking about vocations, younger students were more apt to do so than older students. Slightly less than a third of those who took ACRE1 (31%) indicated thinking at some point about having a vocation, but the numbers drop to less one in five for students who took ACRE2 (17%) and ACRE3 (18%). No meaningful differences exist in the percentages of students from Catholic schools and parish programs regarding their thoughts about vocations.

Table 5.12 Mean Scale Scores
and Percent Agreement to the Vocation Item

	Mean Scores			Strongly Agree / Total Agreement		
Vocation	**ACRE1**	**ACRE2**	**ACRE3**	**ACRE1**	**ACRE2**	**ACRE3**
I have thought about becoming a sister, brother, or priest	2.12	1.76	1.68	8/31	3/17	3/18

Section 2: Comparison of Subscales across Levels by Groups

The figures in this section provide a visual image of the comparison of the average scores of subscales from ACRE1 to ACRE2 to ACRE3 for both Catholic students from Catholic schools and students from parish religious education programs. Figure 5.7 shows the comparison for Catholic school students and Figure 5.8 shows the comparison for students from parish programs.

For Catholic students from Catholic schools (Figure 5.7), a decline in the average scores from ACRE1 to ACRE2 for all subscales and, except for the Catholic identity subscale, the declines continue from ACRE2 to ACRE3. The largest declines occur in moral judgments, Catholic identity, and relationship with Jesus. The decline in moral judgments is attributable to more permissive attitudes on the part of the older students in Catholic high schools toward cheating and the use of drugs, and the inclusion of additional items not present on ACRE1 that concern drinking and cohabitation before marriage (see Figure 5.4). The decline in Catholic identity is a function of a decline in each item, but occurs mostly in the older students' agreement that they participate in the Sacrament of Penance and their agreement to the importance of praying the rosary (see Figure 5.3). Finally, the decline in the Relationship with Jesus subscale is a result of the decline of student responses to two items, that Jesus understands them and that the relationship with Jesus helps them (see Figure 5.1).

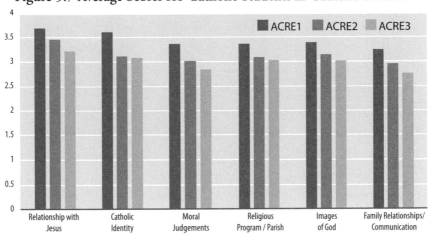

Figure 5.7 Average Scores for Catholic Students in Catholic Schools

The pattern of beliefs, attitudes, perceptions and practices across the levels of ACRE for the students from parish programs is more uniform than for students from Catholic schools (see Figure 5.8). The most noticeable decline for students in parish programs occurs on moral judgments for the same reasons that the decline was evident for Catholic school students: more permissive attitudes toward cheating and the drug usage, and the inclusion of additional items not present on ACRE1 that concern drinking and cohabitation before marriage (see Figure 5.4).

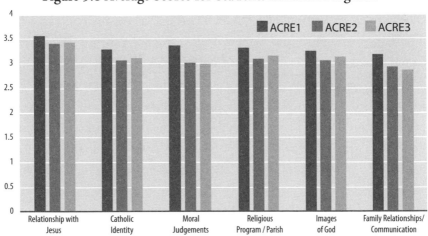

Figure 5.8 Average Scores for Students in Parish Programs

Section 3: Student Perceptions of Problems in their Schools

The final set of items in Part 2 asked the students to identify concerns they have about various issues that they view may be problems in their schools. The students rated each issue according to the following scale: Not a problem, Minor problem or Major problem in their schools. Since the unit of analysis is students and not schools, the percentages reported in this section refer to students and not to schools. Therefore, it would be incorrect to interpret the percentages as the percent of Catholic schools or parish religious education programs that experience the particular problem.

Depending upon the level of ACRE, the students rated from 9 to 13 items in the following eight areas:

Decorum: Cursing (+ blasphemy, swearing); Teasing (+ bullying, name-calling)

Altercations: Fighting

Lack of Honesty: Cheating

Safety: Personal Safety

Substance Abuse: Alcohol; Marijuana; Other drugs

Bias: Racism; Respect for diversity

Sexual Behavior: Sexual harassment; Date rape

Disorders: Eating disorders

The data are reported for students in Catholic schools and those in other schools by each level of ACRE. Students in particular parish religious education programs would likely be attending a variety of schools in which a different set of problems to varying degrees might be present. As a result, it would be expected that the ratings of problems in their schools by students in parish religious education programs would have more variability than the ratings from students in Catholic schools. Even so, the comparison of the average percentages for Catholic schools and other schools would provide a general impression as to the extent each specific issue raised was about the same or more or less prevalent in Catholic schools in comparison to other schools.

Table 5.13 Means[7], Percent Major Problem[8] and Effect Sizes for Perceptions of Problems in Schools

Problem	Catholic Schools		Other Schools[9]		
	Mean	Percent Major Problem	Mean	Percent Major Problem	Effect Size
ACRE1					
Teasing	.580	35%	.606	42%	.07
Cheating	.517	29%	.564	37%	.13
Cursing	.517	34%	.589	44%	.18
Fighting	.468	29%	.537	37%	.17
Drugs	.285	27%	.407	38%	.27
Racism	.281	21%	.363	28%	.20
Alcohol	.277	25%	.391	36%	.28
Respect for Diversity	.187	7%	.214	9%	.09
Personal Safety	.140	6%	.177	9%	.13
ACRE2					
Cursing	.586	32%	.703	52%	.35
Cheating	.570	27%	.645	41%	.24
Teasing	.537	24%	.633	39%	.30
Fighting	.371	13%	.554	31%	.54
Eating Disorders	.258	12%	.399	21%	.39
Racism	.248	17%	.415	28%	.43
Sexual Harassment	.245	17%	.435	30%	.48
Respect for Diversity	.242	12%	.352	17%	.32
Alcohol	.240	14%	.469	29%	.61
Drugs	.226	16%	.474	33%	.63
Marijuana	.219	16%	.458	33%	.61
Date Rape	.179	16%	.315	27%	.35
Personal Safety	.172	8%	.300	14%	.40

Table 5.13 continued

Problem	Catholic Schools		Other Schools[9]		
	Mean	Percent Major Problem	Mean	Percent Major Problem	Effect Size
ACRE3					
Alcohol	.624	44%	.689	51%	.17
Cheating	.617	39%	.658	45%	.12
Cursing	.606	48%	.691	49%	.24
Marijuana	.552	35%	.537	25%	−.04
Drugs	.458	26%	.512	31%	.14
Eating Disorders	.360	17%	.357	14%	−.02
Respect for Diversity	.307	12%	.353	12%	.13
Racism	.299	14%	.393	20%	.26
Fighting	.295	9%	.441	17%	.45
Sexual Harassment	.232	12%	.340	16%	.37
Personal Safety	.185	7%	.245	7%	.19
Date Rape	.159	11%	.208	14%	.15

Relative Seriousness of Problems

Table 5.13 shows the means, the percentage of students who indicated that the problem was a major one in their schools, and the effect sizes of the relative magnitude of problems in their schools as identified by the students at each level of ACRE. As before, the effect size is a measure of the relative size of the

---

[7] The mean is the average score for each problem after the application of the following transformation: 0=Not a Problem, 0.5=A Minor Problem and 1.0=A Major Problem. The mean is an index ranging from 0 to 1 that describes the relative magnitude of the problem in the schools. Higher means indicate the students viewed the issue as more of a problem than those issues with lower means.

[8] This index describes the percentage of students who indicated that the problem was a major one in their schools.

[9] Data are from students in parish religious education programs virtually all of whom do not attend Catholic schools. Exceptions would occur if the parish requires all students to attend the parish program for sacramental preparation, particularly Confirmation. It is not known whether this occurred for the students in this study.

differences between the concerns of students in Catholic schools and those in other schools. Figures 5.9 to 5.12 are based on the data from Table 5.13.

As might be expected, the pattern of the type and magnitude of problems changes according to the level of ACRE. Students who took ACRE1 were in elementary schools, typically the 5th grade. Those Catholic school students who took ACRE2 were usually in the 8th grade of an elementary school, whereas those students from other schools typically were in a middle school or junior high school. The typical student who took ACRE3 was a junior or senior in high school. The students in the lower grades generally reported more problems with decorum, cheating and fighting, whereas students in the upper grades were more likely to report problems with decorum, cheating, and substance abuse.

Figure 5.9 Magnitudes of Problems in Catholic Schools: Decorum, Fighting, Honesty, Safety, Eating Disorders

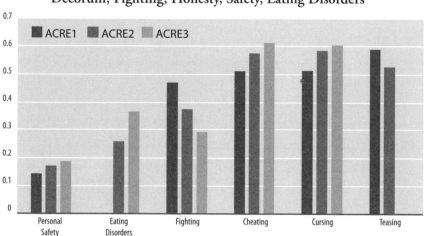

Figure 5.10 Effect Sizes for Decorum, Fighting, Honesty, Safety, Eating Disorders

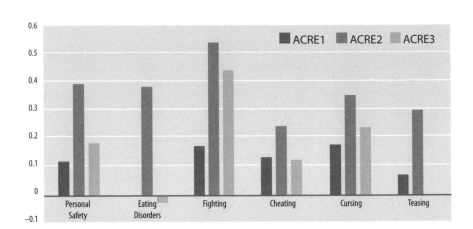

Decorum

Lack of decorum is among the most frequently noted problems by students in the elementary schools (ACRE1 and ACRE2). Over 80 percent of the students from both Catholic schools and other schools report that teasing, along with bullying and name-calling, is at least a minor problem in their schools. Fewer Catholic school students (35% on ACRE1 and 24% on ACRE2) than parish religious education students (42% on ACRE1 and 39% on ACRE2) report that teasing is a major problem in their schools.

Cursing, along with blasphemy and swearing, is also reported as being prevalent in the elementary schools as well as in the high schools, with the older students reporting the problem more frequently than did the younger students. Cursing is reported as a major problem in the schools by about a third of students in Catholic elementary schools and almost half of those in Catholic high schools. The relative occurrence of cursing as denoted by the effect sizes is less prevalent in Catholic schools than in other schools.

Altercations

Fighting also is a common problem encountered in the schools, more so among the younger students than among the older students. Almost two-thirds of the students in Catholic schools who took ACRE1 report at least a minor problem with fighting, compared with 50 percent of the students who took ACRE3. Students in other schools report fighting more frequently as a problem than do students in Catholic schools. Seventy percent of those in parish religious education programs who took ACRE1 and ACRE3 and 80 percent of those who took ACRE2 report fighting to be at least a minor problem in their schools, with between 17 percent (ACRE3) to 37 percent (ACRE1) reporting it to be a major problem. The largest difference in reported fighting by Catholic school students and those in other schools occurs on ACRE2, where most of the Catholic school students are still in elementary schools, whereas the vast majority of students in other schools would be in middle schools or junior high schools.

Lack of Honesty

The students at all three levels of ACRE report that cheating is another problem common in their schools. The concern with cheating increases slightly from ACRE1 to ACRE2 (Figure 5.9); however, the differences between the concerns of students in Catholic schools and those in other schools are not large (Figure 5.10). Approximately, 75 percent of the students on ACRE1 and 85 percent of those on ACRE2 and ACRE3 report a problem with cheating in their schools. A lower percentage of students from Catholic schools than other schools report that cheating is a major problem (29% vs. 37% on ACRE1; 27% vs. 41% on ACRE2; and 39% vs. 45% on ACRE3).

Personal Safety

As shown in Figure 5.9, concern about personal safety is not viewed as a problem in Catholic schools. Approximately three-quarters of the students in Catholic schools report that personal safety is not a problem in their schools (78% on ACRE1, 74% on ACRE2 and 71% on ACRE3). Most students who attended other schools also do not show a great concern about personal safety (73% on ACRE1, 55% on ACRE2 and 58% on ACRE3). As shown by the larger effect size of .40 in Table 5.13 and graphically in Figure 5.10, the students attending other than Catholic schools who took ACRE2 have a much higher concern about personal safety than do their counterparts in Catholic schools.

Eating Disorders

Eating disorders are perceived to be more problematic in high school (ACRE3) than in 8th grade (ACRE2). The largest differences, however, between the concerns of students in Catholic schools and those in other schools occur on ACRE2 (see Figure 5.10). Fifty-nine percent of students who attended other schools report at least a minor problem with eating disorders in the school on ACRE2, compared with forty percent of students in Catholic schools. On ACRE3, 56 percent of students in Catholic schools and 58% of students in others schools report some concern with eating disorders in the schools.

Substance Abuse

Older students more than younger ones report more frequent problems in their schools with alcohol and drugs. Figure 5.11 shows that the rapid increase in the level of concern for students in ACRE3 compared with ACRE1 and ACRE2. Figure 5.12 shows that the discrepancy in the level of concern of students in Catholic schools and those in other schools about substance abuse in their schools is greatest for ACRE2, when most Catholic school students are still in elementary schools and most other students are in junior high or middle schools. Perceptions about the use of alcohol being at least a minor problem increase as the levels of ACRE increase in both Catholic schools (30% on ACRE1, 34% on ACRE2 and 81% on ACRE3) and other schools (42% on ACRE2, 65% on ACRE2, and 87% on ACRE3).

With regard to drugs, less than one-third of the students in Catholic elementary schools (30% on ACRE1 and 28% on ACRE2) view them as a problem in their schools, whereas more than two thirds of the Catholic schools students in high school view them as a school problem (66% thought the use of drugs is at least a minor problem, 75% thought marijuana is at least a minor problem). Students in other schools identify drugs as a problem more than do the students in Catholic schools. The effect sizes range from .14 for ACRE3 to .63 for ACRE2. Marijuana, which is an item on ACRE2 and ACRE3, but not on ACRE1, is seen by students in Catholic schools to be about the same degree of a problem as other drugs in elementary school (ACRE2: marijuana 37%, other drugs 38%), but slightly more of a problem than other drugs in high school (ACRE3: marijuana 75%; other drugs, 66%). Students in other schools, however, report more concerns about other drugs than they do about marijuana (ACRE3: marijuana 62%, other drugs 72%).

Figure 5.11 Magnitudes of Problems in Catholic Schools: Bias, Substance Abuse, Sexual Problems

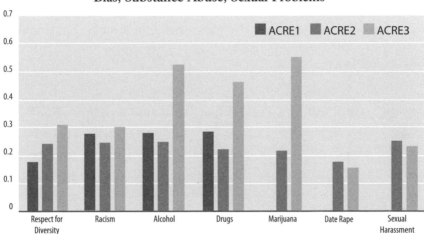

Figure 5.12 Effect Sizes for Bias, Substance Abuse, Sexual Behavior

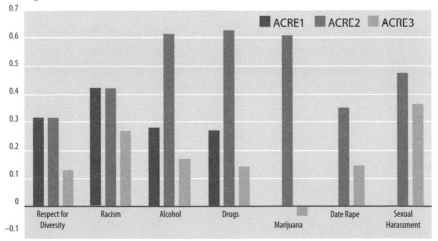

Bias

Perceived problems with respect for diversity increase slightly in the schools from ACRE1 to ACRE3. Concerns about racism, which are slightly more prevalent than concerns about diversity, are fairly uniform across the levels of ACRE. Students attending other than Catholic schools report more issues with both racism and problems with respect for diversity than do the students attending Catholic schools. The differences in issues involving bias between the Catholic schools and other schools are greatest on ACRE2, as indicated by the effect sizes for racism (.43) and respect for diversity (.32). Approximately two-thirds of the students in Catholic elementary schools and about half of those in Catholic high schools report that bias is not a problem in their schools.

Sexual Behavior

The two items on ACRE concerning problems with sexual behavior involve date rape and sexual harassment. These items appear only on ACRE2 and ACRE3. Date rape has the second lowest scaled score (Table 5.13) on ACRE2 and the lowest on ACRE3. The perception of the incidence of date rape, however, is higher in other schools than in the Catholic schools, particularly in the middle schools and junior high schools (Figure 5.12). Sexual harassment, on the other hand, is viewed as more prevalent in the schools. The differences between Catholic schools and other schools on problems with sexual harassment are greater than the differences on problems with date rape. Thirty-one percent of Catholic schools students on ACRE 2 and 33 percent on ACRE3 indicate that sexual harassment is at least a minor problem in their school compared with 57 percent on ACRE2 of students from other schools and 53 percent on ACRE3. On the other hand, 19 percent of Catholic school students on ACRE2 and 20 percent on ACRE3 report that date rape is at least a minor problem compared with 36 percent of students from other schools on ACRE2 and 28 percent on ACRE3.

Summary

Teasing, which includes bullying and name-calling, cursing, cheating, and fighting are identified as most problematic by the students in both Catholic schools and other schools. In virtually all cases, the problems encountered are greater in other schools than in Catholic schools (see Table 5.13). The largest discrepancies between Catholic schools and other schools, as noted by the effect sizes of .40 or larger, are the relative seriousness of problems with alcohol, drugs, racism, fighting, sexual harassment and personal safety. Both Catholic school students and those in other schools report the fewest problems with respect for diversity and personal safety.

The pattern of the relative seriousness of the problems in the high schools (ACRE3) is somewhat different than the pattern present in the elementary schools (ACRE1 and ACRE2). Cheating and cursing remain major issues in the schools, but they are joined by problems with alcohol and drugs for older students. Fighting, sexual harassment, racism and cursing are reported as more prevalent in the other schools attended by students who took ACRE3 than in the Catholic schools.

Chapter 6

Predictors of Faith Knowledge, Mass Attendance, and Relationship with Jesus

Introduction

This chapter contains the results of analyses that identified the most important predictors of students' achievement in faith knowledge, their reported attendance at Mass, and the degree of their reported relationship with Jesus.

In their earlier work on ACRE, Convey and Thompson (1999) had searched for the most important predictors of religious knowledge and religious practice for the students who had taken ACRE in 1995. Their principal findings were as follows:

- A strong relationship existed between religious knowledge and religious practice at each grade level. Religious practice was a slightly more important predictor of religious knowledge than religious knowledge was of religious practice.

- The type of program a student attended (parish-based or school-based) was an important predictor of religious knowledge at all levels of ACRE. Students from Catholic schools scored higher on religious knowledge than did students from parish-based programs. However, the program the student attended was an important predictor of religious practice only for younger students who took ACRE1.

- A student's relationship with Jesus and the indicators of the student's Catholic Identity, as measured by attendance at Mass, participation in the sacraments, devotional practices, and the importance placed on being Catholic were important predictors of both religious knowledge and religious practice.

- A student's relationship with his or her family, as measured by the family praying together, talking to parents about religious and moral matters, and eating meals together, was an important predictor of religious practice, but not of religious knowledge.

- A student's perception of his or her parish was an important predictor of religious knowledge for students taking ACRE2 and ACRE3, but only important for religious practice for students in grades 11 and 12 (ACRE3).

In the current study, the statistical procedure of multiple regression analysis was used to identify the most important predictors of the following three outcome measures:

- Achievement in faith knowledge, as measured by the total score on Part 1;

- Reported agreement to attending Mass on weekends, as measured by a single item on Part 2;

- Relationship with Jesus, as measured by the total score of the four items that constituted the Relationship with Jesus subscale on Part 2.

Nine regression analyses were performed, one for each level of ACRE with each of the three outcome measures. The outcome measures used provide an index of religious knowledge, one form of religious practice (attending Mass on weekends), and a measure of students' relationship with Jesus. Only data from Catholic students are used in these statistical analyses.

The set of variables for the analyses to predict faith knowledge consists of program type (whether the student attended a Catholic school or parish-based religious education program) and all the items in Part 2 of ACRE, except those that ask about perceived problems in the schools. The set of variables for the analyses to predict Mass attendance are the total faith knowledge score, program type, and the remaining items in Part 2. The set of variables for the analyses to predict Relationship with Jesus consists of program type and the items in Part 2 that are not part of the Relationship with Jesus subscale.

The regression analyses proceeded by entering all the predictors in one step. Due to the large number of students in each of the analyses, virtually all predictors are statistically significant, including those that produce only a very small change in prediction. Many of these predictors would not be practically meaningful. As a result, the standardized regression coefficients or *beta* coefficients are used as the measures of the relative importance of the predictor, with larger coefficients indicative of more important predictors.

The tables that follow in this chapter show the results of the regression analyses for the three outcome measures. The numbers in the cells of the tables are the standardized regression (*beta*) coefficients. In addition to program type, only the four or five highest or most important *beta* coefficients are shown. The R^2 in the last row in each of the tables indicates the percentage of the dependent variable in that analysis that is explained by the entire set of predictors in the model, not just those predictors that are reported in the tables.

Prediction of Faith Knowledge

Table 6.1 shows the five most important predictors of achievement in faith knowledge. The percentage of variance explained ranges from 19.5 percent on ACRE3 to 22.6 percent on ACRE2. This range of the percentage of variance explained is about average in the social sciences for predicting achievement from non-achievement predictors.

Three variables consistently emerge as important predictors of faith knowledge across the three levels of ACRE:

- Program type (school-based or parish-based);
- Reported attendance at Mass on the weekends;
- Importance placed on praying the rosary.

The identification of program type as the most important predictor of achievement in faith knowledge for students in ACRE1 and ACRE2 and the second most important predictor for those who took ACRE3 is not unexpected. The results of the analyses in earlier chapters reveal that students in Catholic school scored higher in faith knowledge than did students in parish religious education programs. What the regression analysis does, however, is to control the relative importance of each predictor according to the other predictors in the model. Hence, program type remains an important predictor even controlling for the students' relationship with Jesus, their images of God, moral positions, Catholic practices and devotions, and sentiments toward their parishes and religion programs.

Table 6.1 Most Important Predictors of Faith Knowledge[1]

PREDICTORS	ACRE1	ACRE2	ACRE3
Program Type (School or Parish)	.277	.286	.118
I attend Saturday evening / Sunday Mass	.173	.174	.192
I believe that Jesus cured the blind and raised the dead	.119	.097	—
Praying the rosary is important to me	.122	.153	.132
My religion teachers have been a positive influence on how I think and live	.109	—	—
It is (not) all right for a couple to live together before getting married	—	.084	.134
Our religion program encourages us to do volunteer work	—	—	.088
Percentage of Variance Explained	**20.5%**	**22.6%**	**19.5%**

The student's reported agreement of attending Mass on the weekends is the second most important predictor of achievement in faith knowledge for students on ACRE1 and ACRE2 and the most important predictor for those who took ACRE3. Students with higher levels of agreement that they go to Mass on weekends do better on faith knowledge achievement than do those whose agreement about attending Mass is lower. Students who go to Mass regularly on weekends are more familiar with the parts of the Mass and they may have benefited from the homilies that they heard. In addition, these students are likely to receive more reinforcement and help from their families in understanding the truths of the faith. The emergence of attendance at Mass as an important predictor takes into account the other predictors in the model,

---

[1] The numbers in table are standardized regression coefficients or *beta* coefficients. Only the five highest coefficients are shown for each level of ACRE.

including whether they attend a Catholic school or a parish religious education program.

The importance that students place on praying the rosary is the third of the most important predictors of achievement in faith knowledge common to all three levels of ACRE. Students with higher levels of agreement to the importance of this traditional Catholic devotional practice score higher on faith knowledge than do students with lower levels of agreement. It is important to note that the item does not ask whether the students pray the rosary or how often they do. Rather the item is measuring the sentiments of students regarding the importance of praying the rosary.

The remaining important predictors of achievement in faith knowledge vary from level to level. These predictors are belief in Jesus' miracles (ACRE1, ACRE2), adherence to traditional moral position on cohabitation of couples before marriage (ACRE2, ACRE3), influence of religion teachers (ACRE1) and the encouragement by their religion programs for them to participate in volunteer work (ACRE3).

Prediction of Reported Mass Attendance

Table 6.2 shows in addition to program type and achievement in faith knowledge the five most important predictors of a student's agreement that he or she attends Mass on the weekends. When controlling for program type and the total score on faith knowledge, four variables consistently emerge as important predictors of reported Mass attendance:

- Family praying together at home;
- Participation in the sacrament of Penance;
- Belonging to an excellent parish;
- Importance of being a Catholic.

Those students who report that their lives are influenced by traditional Catholic values show higher levels of agreement to attending Mass on weekends than do those students who report lower levels of influence.

Program type and the total score on faith knowledge are included in
Table 6.2 to illustrate their importance relative to the other predictors of Mass
attendance. Achievement in faith knowledge is an important predictor of Mass
attendance; however, it is not as strong a predictor as the family praying
together. The negative coefficient for program type for ACRE3 is indicative of
students in parish programs reporting higher Mass attendance than students
in Catholic schools.

Table 6.2 Most Important Predictors of Reported Mass Attendance[2]

PREDICTORS	ACRE1	ACRE2	ACRE3
My family prays together at home	.238	.250	.241
I participate in the sacrament of Penance	.101	.115	.121
I think about a vocation	.063	—	—
Being a Catholic is important to me	.049	.068	.117
I belong to an excellent parish	.053	.087	.146
It is (not) all right for a couple to live together before getting married	—	.072	.092
Percentage of Variance Explained	22.4%	30.4%	40.1%
Program Type (School or Parish)	.061	.071	−.053
Faith Knowledge Total Score	.169	.156	.142

The most important predictor of students' agreement that they attend Mass
on weekends is the family praying together at home. Families that pray together
before meals or at other times provide a strong level of support for the religious
practice of their children. Such families also are likely to attend Mass regularly
as a family. The support provided by these families exemplifies what the
sociologist James Coleman has called "social capital" (Coleman, 1988). Social
capital, unlike physical capital (wealth, property, etc.) and human capital
(intelligence, personality, etc), exists in relationships. Research has consistently
found that a high level of social capital is efficacious for children. A key factor

---

[2] The numbers in table are standardized regression coefficients or *beta* coefficients.
In addition to the coefficients for program type and faith knowledge, only the five
highest coefficients for the other predictors are shown for each level of ACRE.

in the development of social capital is the relationship between children and adults. Research has also shown that social capital, which is present in functional communities, communities that work to produce good results, are instrumental to the effectiveness of Catholic schools (Convey, 1992). The primary functional community for children is the family. Strong and supportive relationships with the family produce efficacious social capital. Family relationships that include an explicit spiritual component should result in better religious practice among the children in the family.

Participating in the Sacrament of Penance is among the most important predictors of regular Mass attendance for students. Students with higher levels of agreement to participating in the Sacrament of Penance are more likely to have higher agreement to indicating that they attend Mass on weekends than do students with lower levels of agreement. The finding is important given the decline in participation in the Sacrament of Penance. The item about Penance does not ask about frequency of going to confession, but rather whether the students agree or disagree that they participate in the Sacrament of Reconciliation. It is likely that students in Catholic elementary schools and, to some extent, those in elementary schools and middle schools in parish programs go to confession with their classes periodically. However, the predictor remains strong even when controlling for program type. Therefore, participating in the Sacrament of Penance is a legitimate predictor of Mass attendance in that at least a periodic use of the sacrament is predictive of whether the students attend Mass on weekends.

Belonging to an excellent parish is also among the most important predictors of Mass attendance at all levels of ACRE. Much like supports provided by the functional community of the family, a vibrant and active parish also provides additional support for the spiritual development of young people. It stands to reason that students who find a welcoming environment in Church, feel comfortable at Mass, and have the opportunity to be involved in parish activities will be likely to attend Mass on a regular basis.

The last of the most important predictors of Mass attendance common to each analysis is a student's agreement that being a Catholic is important. It is clear from the analyses that students who feel that Catholicism is important to them are acting upon their convictions and are fulfilling their responsibilities as Catholics by attending Mass on a regular basis.

The two remaining items that emerge as important predictors of reported Mass attendance vary from level to level. For ACRE1, thinking about a vocation is an important predictor of Mass attendance. On ACRE2 and ACRE3, subscribing to the traditional moral position on cohabitation of couples before marriage, an item that is also an important predictor of the achievement of faith knowledge, is among the five most important predictors of Mass attendance.

Prediction of Relationship with Jesus

Table 6.3 shows in addition to the student's program the five most important variables for each level of ACRE that predict students' reported relationship with Jesus. The items in Part 2 that constitute the Relationship with Jesus sub-scale are excluded from the predictor set. As was the case when attendance at Mass was the outcome variable, program type is also included in Table 6.3; however, in this case it turns out not to be among the tops predictors of a student's relationship with Jesus. The variance explained in these models is the highest of the three outcome variables, ranging from 47.8 percent for ACRE1 to 69.9 percent for ACRE3.

The following four variables consistently emerge as important predictors of the students reported relationship with Jesus:

- Believing that God listens to their prayers;
- Believing that God loves them even when they sin;
- Believing that God speaks to them through the Bible;
- Being a Catholic is important.

The two remaining important predictors of reported relationship with Jesus are the importance of praying the rosary (ACRE1, ACRE2) and a desire to learn how to get closer to God (ACRE3).

Table 6.3 Most Important Predictors of Relationship with Jesus[3]

PREDICTORS	ACRE1	ACRE2	ACRE3
One way that God speaks to me is through the Bible	.184	.156	.134
When I pray, God really does listen to me	.155	.203	.231
Even when I sin, God still loves me	.138	.202	.193
Being a Catholic is important to me	.134	.179	.171
Praying the rosary is important to me	.110	.097	—
I would like to learn how to get closer to God	—	—	.185
Percentage of Variance Explained	47.8%	60.6%	69.9%
Program Type (School or Parish)	.047	.020	.004

Most of the important predictors of a student's relationship with Jesus are measures of the student's image of God. From a theological, practical and psychometric point of view, the similarity of the constructs "God" and "Jesus" likely account for the high amount of variance explained in the three regression models. Students who have positive images of God, who would like to get closer to God, and who believe that God listens to them when they pray and that God loves them even when they sin also perceive themselves to have a favorable relationship with Jesus.

The importance of being a Catholic also is an important predictor of one's relationship with Jesus for students at all levels of ACRE. This finding demonstrates that students likely have grasped the centrality of the person of Jesus to Catholicism. Indeed, teaching about Jesus and his message is one of the principal tasks of religious instruction and catechesis. Finally, the students' agreement that praying the rosary is also among the most important predictors of the relationship with Jesus for students who were not yet in high school (ACRE1 and ACRE2). Students who agree that praying the rosary is important for them also are more likely to score higher on the Relationship with Jesus subscale.

---

[3] The numbers in table are standardized regression coefficients or *beta* coefficients. In addition to the coefficients for program type and faith knowledge, only the five highest coefficients for the other predictors are shown for each level of ACRE.

Summary

As Convey and Thompson had found in 1999, this study also shows that the prediction of the sentiment outcomes, particularly students' agreement that they attend Mass on weekends and their reported relationship with Jesus, is better than the prediction of faith knowledge (religious knowledge). Also consistent with the findings of Convey and Thompson, whether students receive their religious instruction in school-based or parish-based programs is an important predictor of faith knowledge and the most important for students taking ACRE1 and ACRE2. However, whether students are in school-based or parish-based programs is less important in predicting Mass attendance and the students' reported relationship with Jesus.

One striking finding common to all three prediction models is the importance of a set of predictors that basically measure traditional Catholic values and practices. These predictors are attending Mass on a regular basis, praying the rosary, praying together as a family, participating in the Sacrament of Penance, and the importance to the students of being a Catholic. In general, when it comes to behavior and sentiments, children raised in an environment that supports these traditional Catholic values will do better than other children regardless in what setting they received their religious education. On the other hand, the evidence from this study shows that with regard to knowing about the faith, at least in those aspects measured by ACRE, children in Catholic schools will have a better understanding of their faith than children who receive their religious education in parish-based programs.

Chapter 7
Summary, Conclusions and Recommendations

This chapter presents a summary of the findings regarding students' knowledge of the faith and their beliefs, attitudes, practices and perceptions across the three levels of ACRE. The performance of the students on specific themes is discussed and recommendations are presented.

Summary of Findings

- ACRE has sufficient reliability and content validity (mapping to *The Protocol for Assessing the Conformity of Catechetical Materials with the Catechism of the Catholic Church*) to make it an effective assessment for measuring catechetical outcomes.

- Students in Catholic schools, both Catholics and non-Catholics, score higher on faith knowledge than do students from parish programs. The differences in the achievement on faith knowledge between Catholics in Catholic schools and those in parish programs are larger on ACRE1 and ACRE 2 than they are on ACRE3.

- With some exceptions by level, students score best on the domains relating to God and the Church and poorest on the domains relating to relating to Morality, Literacy, and Church History.

- Items on which students have the lowest achievement are just as likely to concern basic literacy about the faith as more theoretical and technical theological distinctions.

- A slight decline in the average level of agreement to items measuring beliefs, attitudes, practices and perceptions is evident for older students when compared with younger students.

- The beliefs, attitudes, practices and perceptions of students in Catholic schools and those in parish program are similar for virtually all items on ACRE1 and ACRE2. More differences in beliefs, attitudes, practices and perceptions occur on ACRE3, where high school students in parish programs generally have higher or more favorable average agreement than do students in Catholic high schools.

- Students at all levels show a high level of agreement to items relating to their relationship with Jesus and their images of God.

- Students in Catholic schools report a lower occurrence in their schools of problems with deportment, honesty, substance abuse, harassment, and safety than students in parish programs report about their schools. The frequency in the occurrence of problems between Catholic schools and other schools are higher for the schools attended by older students than for those attended by younger students.

- The most frequently occurring problems in their schools reported by students in elementary schools are cursing, cheating and teasing. For high schools, the most frequent problems reported are with alcohol, cheating, cursing, marijuana and other drugs.

- The best predictors of achievement in faith knowledge are the type of program in which the students are enrolled (Catholic schools do better) and reported attendance at Mass. Other important predictors are importance of praying the rosary, belief in Jesus' miracles, proper moral sense about cohabitation prior to marriage, and influences of the religion program (influence of a teacher or encouragement to volunteer).

- The best predictors of Mass attendance are family praying together at home and participation in the Sacrament of Reconciliation. Other important predictors are belonging to an excellent parish, the importance of being a Catholic, belief in Jesus' miracles, and the proper moral sense about cohabitation prior to marriage. The type of program in which the students enrolled is not a predictor of Mass attendance.

- The best predictors of Relationship with Jesus are students' images of God, the importance of being a Catholic, and the importance of praying the rosary. The type of program in which the students enrolled is not a predictor of Relationship with Jesus.

The Central Role of Christology

A primary purpose of catechesis is to teach about Jesus Christ and his role in the salvation of the world. As the Catechism of the Catholic Church states, "to catechize is 'to reveal in the Person of Christ the whole of God's eternal design. . . to seek to understand the meaning of Christ's actions . . .'" (*CCC*, 426).

The results from this study indicate that, for the most part, those Catholic students who participate in formal religious instruction in Catholic schools and in parish programs have a good understanding of the person of Jesus and his salvific mission. They understand that Jesus is one person with a human nature and a divine nature. They recognize the significance of his death and resurrection. The students generally have favorable images of Jesus, believing in his miracles, viewing him as their savior and friend, and recognizing his welcoming approach to sinners. The vast majority of students feel that Jesus understands them and that their relationship with him really helps them.

These results suggest that, at least for the students in this study, their teachers and catechists individually and in conjunction with the reinforcement they receive from priests in homilies and parents at home are having some success getting across the message about Jesus and his works. These results also are in accord with those of previous studies of ACRE (Convey & Thompson, 1999) and its predecessor, REKAP and REOI (Thompson, 1982).

The Trinity

Many Catholic students in this study do not have an adequate understanding of the Church's teaching about the Trinity. Only slightly more than 50 percent of the students who took ACRE2 recognize the Trinity as the central mystery of Christian faith and life. In addition, many students do not understand that the Trinity is one God in three persons. Rather than identifying the Father, Son and Holy Spirit as three persons in one God, approximately a third of the students who took ACRE2 and almost 20 percent who took ACRE 3 thought that the three persons of the Trinity represent three Gods. Finally, the students have the most problems with the identification of the Holy Spirit as the third Person of the Trinity and the role of the Spirit in the Church. Almost a third of students who took ACRE1 in Catholic schools and slightly less than one-half of those in parish programs answered items about the Holy Spirit incorrectly.

Knowledge of Scripture

Most students in this study understand that the Bible is the inspired Word of God. Many students are also familiar with biblical passages that are commonly used at Mass or may even appear in their literature books. A good example is the parable of the Prodigal Son. The students know the "big picture" about scripture; however, they have varying degrees of difficulty with many of the details relating to scripture that they might be expected to know. For example, many students do not have a clear idea as to the content of the Old Testament and the New Testament, the purpose of Jesus' parables, the nature of the Acts of the Apostles, and when the Gospels were written and by whom. Younger students in the study, those who took ACRE1, demonstrate little notion of the meaning of covenant in the Old Testament; however, the understanding of covenant improves as the children continue in their religious education. Finally, a significant number of students do not understand the dual role of scripture and tradition as sources of revelation. For example, on ACRE3 only 41 percent of those in Catholic schools and one-fourth of those in parish programs correctly identified tradition as a source of revelation.

Sacraments and Liturgy

More than items for any other domain, the achievement of the students in this study on items pertaining to the sacraments and the liturgy is influenced by whether the student reported attending Mass on weekends. Students who reported higher agreement to their attendance at Mass on Saturday evenings or Sundays are more likely than other students to answer correctly items that pertain to the Mass and its parts. Students who report agreement to attending

Mass on weekends better recognize the common prayers of the Mass, such as the Lord's Prayer and the Nicene Creed, than do other students. The students who attend Mass are more familiar with scriptural readings heard during the Liturgy of the Word, such as the parables of the Good Samaritan and the Prodigal Son. These students also have a better understanding than do other students of the major parts of the liturgical year, such as Advent and Ordinary Time, and their significance. They are also more familiar with the concept of the Catechumenate, which they would have encountered at Mass during various parts of the liturgical year. Lastly, they demonstrate more understanding of the Mass as the most important act of worship than do students who report not attending Mass as often on weekends.

The students in the study have a good understanding of the nature of a sacrament. They understand the importance of the sacraments of initiation, with older students showing better understanding than younger students. They show better understanding of some sacraments (e.g., Reconciliation) more than others (e.g., Holy Orders). Many students, however, do not understand the significance of the Paschal Mystery, perhaps because it's a more abstract concept, and its relationship to the sacramental and liturgical life of the Church.

Virtually all students in the study who were asked the question about the nature of the Real Presence understand that Jesus' body and blood are present under the appearances of bread and wine. However, most students do not recognize transubstantiation as the name of the doctrine that refers to the Real Presence of Jesus in the Eucharist. Rather, half the students identify the doctrine either as the Transfiguration or the Incarnation.

Meaning of Major Feasts

Substantial confusion exists among the students in this study about the meanings of the mysteries commemorated by the majors feast days of the Church. Virtually none of the major feasts escapes being misidentified by a significant number of students. Students who report attending Mass on weekends, however, generally do better on identifying the meaning and significance of major feasts than do students who don't attend Mass regularly.

The feasts that celebrate some aspect of Mary's life are particularly problematic, especially the Immaculate Conception. Many students misidentified the feast of the Immaculate Conception as celebrating Mary's virginity rather than her conception without sin. Many students also confuse the meanings of the feasts of the Assumption and the Ascension, identifying the Assumption as signifying Jesus ascending into heaven and the Ascension as the event in which Mary was taken into heaven when her earthly life was ended. Finally, a number of students in this study thought that Catholics celebrate Jesus ascending into heaven on the feast of the Resurrection and that Pentecost Sunday celebrates the baptism of Jesus.

Morality

Most students in the study recognize that they are responsible for making the world a better place. Most also report that they take time to think about whether their actions are right or wrong. The vast majority of students acknowledge that abortion is always wrong under any condition and that it is not all right to try drugs, drink alcohol at a party or cheat by copying homework. Most believe that it is important not to engage in sexual activity before marriage; however, almost three fourths of the students would allow a couple to live together before getting married.

In addition, the students in the study generally have a good understanding of Catholic Social Teaching. Except for their understanding of the meaning of "preferential option for the poor," the students generally achieved high scores on their recognition of the basis for Catholic Social Teaching, their responsibility to care for God's creation, and the life and dignity of the human person. Other components of the domain of Catholic Social Teaching (call to family, community and participation; dignity of work and rights of workers; and solidarity) are not directly assessed by ACRE.

Many students in the study do not have a good understanding of sin. In particular, many do not understand the role of intentionality in sin; that is, to sin is "to choose deliberately" (CCC, 1874). A significant number of the younger students in the study on ACRE1 identify sin as choosing something wrong by accident or making a mistake. The older students in the study have better understanding of the necessity of intentionality for a sin to occur and the proper role of conscience.

Church History and Basic Literacy

The understanding of the students in the study of the items relating to Church History and basic literacy about the faith is mixed. In general, students recognize the responsibilities of the baptized. They understand the reasons to honor Mary and they recognize her role as the Mother of the Church. They know the marks of the church and they understand the nature of the Church's teaching authority, although few of them recognize the word Magisterium or know its meaning.

On the other hand, a number of students in the study have trouble with the meaning of ecumenism, the definition of the communion of saints, and the nature of the Easter Obligation. Many of the younger students in the study fail to understand the role of a bishop.

With regard to Church History, many students lack knowledge of the timing of Vatican Council II and what it accomplished. In addition, the students have deficiencies in their knowledge of historical events and persons, such as the Council of Nicea, St. Thomas Aquinas and the Summa Theologica, Constantine's contributions to Christianity, and the Reformation.

Catholic Schools and Parish Programs

The students in the study from Catholic schools have higher faith knowledge achievement scores than do the students from parish-based programs (confer Table 2.2 in Chapter 2). This finding is not unexpected given that students in Catholic schools receive more instructional time in religion than do students in parish-based programs. Students in Catholic schools typically participate in formal religion classes daily or at least several times a week, while students in parish religious education programs, on average, receive one hour of formal religious instruction per week.

The difference in the nature of religious instruction in Catholic schools and in parish programs was clearly stated in the letter from the Congregation for Catholic Education issued in Vatican City on September 8, 2009. An excerpt from the letter follows:

> "Religious education in schools fits into the evangelizing mission of the Church. It is different from, and complementary to, parish catechesis and other activities such as family Christian education or initiatives of ongoing formation of the faithful. Apart from the different settings in which these are imparted, the aims that they pursue are also different; catechesis aims at fostering personal adherence to Christ and the development of Christian life in its different aspects..., whereas religious education in schools gives the pupils knowledge about Christianity's identity and Christian life." (Religious Education in Schools Fits Into the Evangelizing Mission of the Church, No. 17).

Students in Catholic schools also are taught by experienced teachers, many of whom have graduate degrees and diocesan certification for teachers of religion. On the other hand, virtually all students in parish religious education programs are taught by well-meaning, but inexperienced and likely uncertified teachers who are volunteers. In addition, students in Catholic schools can benefit from the opportunities that their teachers in other subjects take to integrate Catholic teachings into their courses to the extent that it is possible and appropriate. Catholic school students are also in an environment of a faith community where prayer is a daily occurrence and liturgies frequently occur.

A critical factor in learning any subject is the amount of time spent on the subject, which research for years has shown to be predictive of achievement. In 1963, the psychologist John Carroll proposed a model to account for school learning, with the major premise being that school learning is a function of the amount of time spent on a subject (Carroll, 1963). Common sense would yield the same conclusion: the more instructional time spent on a subject, the better one's command of the subject should be. Students in Catholic schools spend approximately five times the amount of time on religion classes than do students in parish programs. Of course, what matters is what is taught in those classes and how it is taught, hence the importance of the teacher, the curriculum and the teacher's knowledge of the subject all interacting in consort.

The question that arises, however, is whether even more should be expected of Catholic school students regarding their knowledge of the faith given the extended time of their religious instruction compared with students in parish religious education programs. Are the Catholic schools doing a good enough job in teaching the faith? Should not more than 20 to 25 percent of students in Catholic schools be scoring at advanced levels (see Table 2.4 in Chapter 2)? And is the threshold score of approximately 64 percent high enough to demonstrate "proficiency" in knowledge of the faith? In school settings in other subjects, typically 64 percent would represent, if not a failing grade, at best a "D."

When it comes to aspects of religious practice, however, students in Catholic schools and those in parish-based programs differ only on a few selected outcomes (confer Table 2.6 in Chapter 2). Most of the differences in measures of beliefs, attitudes, perceptions and practices when they occur favor students in parish-based programs, particularly when the differences occur among the high school students who took ACRE3. This finding is not unexpected since high school parish-based programs tend to attract students who are active in their parishes and have strong family support. The results from the prediction of faith knowledge and religious practice show the importance of the family and the parish in supporting the religious practices of the students.

Findings from the Earlier Research

How different are these findings from those in studies that used data from the earlier version of ACRE and its predecessors? The findings in this study regarding the religious knowledge and sentiments of elementary and high school students are generally consistent with those from the earlier analyses of ACRE, REOI and REKAP. Both Thompson (1982) and Convey and Thompson (1999) found that students were particularly knowledgeable on items that referred to Christ, the Sacraments, Mary, the Church, and Morality, and weak in their knowledge and understanding of religious terminology. A significant finding in this study and in both earlier studies is the number of students who indicated they had a close relationship with Christ and the importance of that relationship as a predictor of religious knowledge and religious practice. Another important finding in this study and earlier studies is the significance of the influence of the family as a predictor of the student's religious practice.

On the other hand, knowledge of traditional theological or religious terminology is a weak area for many students. Thompson (1982) found that only about half of high school students understood the terms Incarnation, Paschal Mystery and revelation. Convey and Thompson (1999) found that a substantial number of students did not know the meaning and significance of Advent, Pentecost, the Immaculate Conception, and the Incarnation. This study has similar findings.

Thus, it appears as though not much has changed over the past 25 years, at least as to the performance of students on similar inventories. Why is this? Is the assessment the problem or is it truly lack of essential knowledge about the Faith? And, if the latter, why has the instruction in the faith not been able to overcome these deficiencies? More studies are needed to address these important questions.

Recommendations

The recommendations are divided into four areas: preparation of catechists, providing a more intentional catechesis, improving and using the assessment of faith knowledge, and suggestions for further research on ACRE.

Preparation of Catechists

The most important factors in teaching children about their faith are the catechist's knowledge and quality of her or his teaching, whether that individual is a classroom teacher, a professional religious educator, a volunteer catechist in a parish program, or a parent instructing his or her children at home. Are those involved in the catechetical ministry adequately prepared to teach and is their preparation up to date? Do they use the latest instructional strategies and technological advances in their teaching? Are they even aware of what is available? Dioceses, parishes and schools should make every effort to provide the supports necessary to ensure that catechists have the requisite knowledge and skills to communicate about the faith effectively with students. The continuous improvement of catechists should be a major priority.

- All dioceses should require catechetical certification for full-time catechists in parish programs and teachers of religion in Catholic schools. Many dioceses already have certification programs and those that don't should institute them. Dioceses should make certification mandatory through the program or through some approved alternative, such as obtaining a graduate degree in theology or religious studies from a Catholic university.

- Schools and parishes, in collaboration with diocesan offices and local Catholic colleges, should increase the professional development opportunities for religion/theology teachers in Catholic schools and catechists in parish programs. The topics for the professional development programs should cover effective teaching strategies and use of technology in addition to catechetical content.

- Parishes should increase the number of full-time professional catechists in the parish so that they can mentor and assist the volunteer catechists who teach the majority of students in the parish religion program. The professional catechist should be a master teacher who has a graduate degree in theology or religious studies and the skills needed to prepare effectively the parents, young adults and others who volunteer to teach in the parish religious education program.

More Intentional Catechesis

The gaps in students' knowledge of their faith are clearly documented in the current study and in previous studies. A more intentional catechesis is necessary by all who are involved with the religious education of young people: classroom teachers, parish catechists, youth ministers, priests and parents. The key word is "intentional," targeted to areas of demonstrated weakness while at the same time reinforcing areas of demonstrated strength. Without a concerted effort in formal catechesis with the allocation of resources needed to accomplish it, the Church risks having an increasing number of Catholics whose illiteracy about the faith is high.

- The United States Conference of Catholic Bishops should produce a curriculum framework for the development of catechetical materials for students in elementary school similar to their framework for high school students, published in July 2008: *Doctrinal Elements for a Curriculum Framework for the Development of Catechetical Materials for Young People of High School Age*. The framework for high school students includes prescribed and optional units on many of the areas in which the results of ACRE show that high school students are weak. A curriculum framework for elementary schools would provide invaluable guidance to publishers in their preparation of resources and to classroom teachers and parish catechists in planning their lessons.

- The United States Conference of Catholic Bishops and the National Catholic Educational Association, in collaboration with the major publishers of Catholic textbooks, should review textbooks and other resources currently in use to determine the extent to which they cover the principal content areas assessed by ACRE and are in conformity with *The Protocol for Assessing the Conformity of Catechetical Materials with the Catechism of the Catholic Church*.

- Priests should include more catechetical material in their homilies. Cardinal William Levada in a conference on doctrine, scripture and preaching in the Church held in Indiana in February 2008 noted that the trend to eliminate catechetical homilies after Vatican II was not intended by *Dei Verbum*, the document on divine revelation from Vatican Council II[1]. He indicated that *Dei Verbum* emphasized the sciptural aspect of the homily because it had been so lacking prior to Vatican II. Priests in their homilies should attempt to include teaching about doctrinal and moral matters in their commentary on the readings for the day. Perhaps, as Carl Anderson, the Supreme Knight of the Knights of Columbus, recommended at a news conference on November 6, 2008 in Ohio, priests should attempt more often to provide

---

[1] Catholic News Service Summary retrieved from USCCB Web site on February 22, 2008.

a linkage between the scripture readings at Sunday Mass and the *Catechism of the Catholic Church.*

- Catholic schools and parish religious education programs should make greater efforts to expose students to scripture, particularly the New Testament. A goal would be to arrange the curriculum so that students, particularly those in Catholic schools where more time is devoted to the teaching of religion, read a substantial part of the New Testament over the course of their schooling.

- In order to increase the basic literacy of the faith, parishes and Catholic schools around the time of each major feast day of the Church should take the time to explain to parishioners and students the meaning of feast and the theological importance of the mystery or event that the feast commemorates.

- Teachers in Catholic schools who do not teach religion should look for opportunities to integrate Catholic teachings into their subjects, wherever possible and appropriate. A Catholic school's Catholic identity is strengthened when education in the faith is supported not only by the formal religion classes, but also by the school's faith community and the intentional integration of Catholic teachings into other parts of the curriculum.

Improving and Using the Assessment

The final set of recommendations concern the assessment itself and its use, particularly in looking forward to the time when ACRE is revised.

- When revising ACRE, the developers should review the goals and specific objectives for each domain to determine whether the operational definitions of the domain are specific enough to provide the desired level of uniformity in emphasis across each of the levels of ACRE. Clearly defined operational definitions will also provide more guidance to item writers and enhance the content validity of ACRE.

- The developers of a revised ACRE should review the annual performance of students on the items on the current form of ACRE to determine whether the items are functioning as intended. In so doing, unintended difficulties with items, such as the item on the theological virtue of hope where the differences in wording resulted in a more difficult item on ACRE1 than on ACRE3, can be avoided, thus improving the assessment.

- The developers of a revised ACRE should include a set of items that is common to all three levels of ACRE. A common set of items, referred to in the assessment literature as an anchor test, can be used to develop linkages between the levels of ACRE in order to facilitate the monitoring of students' growth in their knowledge of their faith.

- When revising ACRE, the developers should consider the appropriateness of using the same strongly agree – strongly disagree scale for all items in Part 2. If all the items in Part 2 are considered as sentiments, then the scale currently in use would be appropriate. If the developers intend to measure a behavior, such as attendance at Mass on weekends, not as a sentiment but rather the extent to which students actually exhibited the behavior, a frequency scale would be more appropriate and would provide less ambiguous and more interpretable information than measuring students' sentiments about the behavior.

- Diocesan offices should encourage a wider use of ACRE and similar assessments as diagnostic tools to identify curricular areas that require more attention in Catholic schools and parish religious education programs. In so doing, classroom teachers, parish catechists and priests in their homilies can target their instruction to help students with their knowledge and understanding of their faith.

Further Research on ACRE

- An item analysis of each level of ACRE should be conducted on an annual basis to determine the stability of the items from year to year. The analysis could use the entire set of examinees each year or a smaller representative random sample of examinees.

- NCEA should consider making the data from ACRE available to researchers and graduate students for use in their dissertations provided that the data are coded in a manner to protect the anonymity and confidentiality to dioceses, schools, parishes and students.

- NCEA should seek funding to support an analysis of the ACRE data that would identify schools and parish programs that are consistently successful in producing good results. These schools and parishes could then be further studied to determine why they are being successful so that best practices could be identified and promoted.

Appendix A
Reliability of ACRE

Reliability of ACRE Part 1

The most relevant form of reliability for ACRE is its internal consistency, the extent to which the performance of examinees on similar items within ACRE is similar. For Part 1 of ACRE, similarity refers to the likelihood that an examinee who answers one item correctly will answer a similar item correctly.

A common measure of internal consistency is a coefficient that is attributed to Lee Cronbach and hence named Cronbach's Alpha or Coefficient Alpha. Coefficient Alpha is a function of both the relationship among the items in a scale, as measured by the average correlation of examinees' responses to the items, and the number of items in the scale. Longer scales generally have higher reliability than shorter scales.

A common standard of acceptability for a reliability coefficient is .80 for a test or scale that has at least 40 items. If a test has fewer than 40 items, a formula known as Spearman-Brown can be used to estimate what the reliability of the test would be if additional items like the ones already on the test were added to bring it up to approximately 40 items (Nunnally, 1978).

Table A.1 shows the internal consistency reliability coefficients for the total scores and the domain scores on Part 1. The total number of items for all three levels of ACRE exceeds 40, so the criterion of .80 is used as the standard of acceptability for the total faith knowledge score for each level. As noted in the table, the standard is exceeded in each case as the reliability coefficients range from .867 for ACRE1 to .902 for ACRE 3.

Since the number of items in each domain for ACRE is well short of 40, the Spearman-Brown Formula is used to establish the lowest acceptable reliability coefficient for scales that range between 5 and 10 items. Except for

Domain 5 Life in Christ (Spearman-Brown Coefficient = .794), the reliability coefficients for each of the domains would exceed .80 if additional items similar to those in the domain were added to bring the number of items up to 40 in each domain. Thus, with this one exception, which is barely under the standard of .80, the faith knowledge domain scores in addition to the total scores on ACRE1, ACRE2 and ARCE3 have sufficient reliability.

Table A.1 Reliability for the Total Score and Domain Scores for Faith Knowledge

	ACRE1		ACRE2		ACRE3	
	Alpha	Items	Alpha	Items	Alpha	Items
Total Score	.867	51	.901	57	.920	63
Domains						
God—Father, Son and Holy Spirit	.413	6	.549	7	.655	8
Church—One, Holy, Catholic, Apostolic	.348	5	.571	8	.593	8
Liturgy and Sacraments	.617	9	.561	8	.592	7
Revelation, Scripture and Faith	.522	7	.563	6	.601	8
Life in Christ—Personal Morality / Catholic Social Teaching	.403	7	.654	10	.603	10
Church History	.331	4	.518	6	.592	8
Prayer / Religious Practices	.379	6	.357	5	.596	8
Catholic Faith Literacy	.491	7	.527	7	.558	6

Reliability of ACRE Part 2

Table A.2 shows the reliability coefficients for each of the subscales of ACRE Part 2. For Part 2 of ACRE, reliability refers to the likelihood that examinees will respond in a similar fashion to items believed to be measuring the same or related concepts. Despite having relatively few items in each, these subscales have substantial levels of reliability and each would exceed the standard of .80 with the application of the Spearman-Brown Formula.

Table A.2 Reliability Coefficients for Subscale Scores on ACRE Part 2

Subscale	ACRE1		ACRE2		ACRE3	
	Alpha	Items	Alpha	Items	Alpha	Items
Relationship with Jesus	.697	4	.816	4	.882	4
Images of God	.453	5	.557	5	.696	6
Catholic Identity	.643	4	.727	4	.795	4
Morality	.340	3	.698	6	.736	6
Family Relationships / Communication	.486	3	.623	4	.595	4
Religion Program / Parish	.695	6	.745	6	.727	6

Appendix B
Examples of Best Practices

Contributors

Sister M. Jane Carew, OV
Director of Religious Education
Diocese of Fort Wayne-South Bend, Indiana

Brian A. Lemoi
Director of the Office of Evangelization and Lifelong Faith Formation
Diocese of St. Petersburg, Florida

Sister Bernadette McManigal, BVM
Superintendent of Schools
Diocese of Arlington, Virginia

Sister Immaculata Paisant, MSC
Superintendent of Catholic Schools
Diocese of Houma-Thibodaux, Louisiana

Alison J. Smith
Coordinator of Religious Education
St. Julie Billiart Parish
Hamilton, Ohio

Karen Vogtner
Principal
St. John the Evangelist School
Hapeville, Georgia

Catholic School Faith Formation
Diocese of Fort Wayne – South Bend, Indiana

The Diocese of Fort Wayne-South Bend located in northeastern Indiana currently has a Catholic population of about 160,000. The Catholic roots of the diocese were established by the missionary labors of French priests and religious sisters who established early foundations of Catholic education. Particularly noteworthy were Father Edward Sorin and his companions who founded the University of Notre Dame in 1844. Recently canonized St. Mother Theodore Guerin and her founding Sisters of Providence came from France in 1840. Following the rivers, Mother Guerin and her sisters eventually came to Fort Wayne in 1845 and established the first of three Catholic schools, two of which still are among the present 39 elementary schools. The diocese has four flourishing Catholic high schools. The total number of teachers is 900, with 3,217 high school students and 9,795 elementary school students.

In 1985 Bishop John M. D'Arcy from the Archdiocese of Boston was installed as the eighth bishop of the Diocese of Fort Wayne – South Bend. During his first year he spent time getting to know his priests, parishes, and the departments that assisted him in his ministry. During his second year he had each of his Chancery departments evaluated by teams of two or three people who came for several days and provided him with objective critiques and advice. The team invited to evaluate the religious education component of parish and schools included Monsignor Francis Kelly and his associate, Wayne Smith of the Religious Education Department at the National Catholic Education Association, and Sister M. Jane Carew, an experienced catechist from the Archdiocese of Boston. Over a period of three days the team visited with Directors of Religious Education and high school religion teachers, principals, parents and pastors in both the Fort Wayne and South Bend areas. At the end of these visits a thorough report was given to Bishop D'Arcy, who afterwards appointed Sister Jane as Director of Religious Education in 1987.

Bishop D'Arcy gave the Office of Religious Education a mandate to provide catechetical formation for parish programs and Catholic schools. One of his major concerns was to strengthen the four high school religion departments. Faith formation was a further mandate for all teachers in the Catholic schools, elementary and high. Informed Catholic teachers, he believed, would bring Catholic principles and identity into all academic subjects. Bishop D'Arcy set a precedent that he would spend a day each spring visiting each of the high schools, meeting with religion teachers and a select group of other teachers and students and visiting a number of the religion classes. The focus of these visits was intended to affirm the positive and improve areas of concern.

In 1989 the Bishop obtained a $320,000 grant from Our Sunday Visitor Publishing Company with the intention of providing all teachers of high school religion with an MA in Theology. Several universities were interviewed and it was decided in 1990 that the University of Dayton would be chosen to provide theological formation to teachers of high school religious education and others in leadership. In 2002 the program was transferred to the University of Notre Dame under the direction of Dr. John Cavadini of its Theology Department.

The Office of Religious Education evaluated teachers and screened potential teachers of religion through interviews and recommendations using the *Catholic School Teacher Perceiver Indicator* from Gallup, Inc. Teachers were chosen based on their teaching potential and their commitment to teaching in concert with the Magisterium of the Church. They were then recommended to the Bishop for canonical appointment in accord with Canon 805.

All teachers were required to attend the *Institute of Catechetical Formation*, a day of instruction sponsored by the diocese. The first Institute Day began in Fall 1988 with an attendance of 700. This particular event included both teachers in Catholic schools and parish catechists. The first keynote speaker, then Father and later Cardinal, Avery Dulles, SJ, emphasized the integrity of content in religious instruction, a central focus of Bishop D'Arcy's vision. During the following seven years, two Institute Days for the Catholic School teachers were held each year, one in Fall and one in Spring in both Fort Wayne and South Bend. By 1995, the format of two Institute Days each year was altered to incorporate one Institute Day and other optional events. These options focus on particular catechetical needs in the elementary schools. Teachers of various grade levels gather to discuss the content of their grade level and gain insight for difficult areas of the curriculum.

Over the years a very strong collaborative relationship developed between the Catholic Schools Office and the Office of Catechesis. These two Offices have a day-long meeting three times a year. Progress is assessed and weaknesses addressed. The collaboration has been a significant witness to principals and teachers affirming faith formation. A teacher from each elementary school is chosen to represent the concerns of faith formation. They attend meetings with the Office of Catechesis to assist the principal in ongoing formation. Another opportunity offered to teachers has been specialized workshops which focus on a particular area such as teaching prayer or sacraments.

The introduction of full-time religion teachers for Grades 6, 7 and 8 has been very positive for the Catholic elementary schools. Some teachers have their MA in Theology. Others have been trained and certified through a diocesan two year program, *Education for Ministry*.

This use of ACRE began in the mid-1990s for four grades. Teachers are told never to 'teach the test' prior to its administration but rather 'teach to the test' throughout the year. In the present curriculum revision the ACRE content is included at each grade level. There is increased focus on vocabulary. All terminology learned in earlier grades are reviewed each year along with the new terms at each grade level. The elementary schools and high school in the diocese collectively score above the national average, some well above the national average.

For the past eight years the use of the Information for Growth (IFG), which is also published by NCEA, has been helpful. The IFG is given to new teachers to assess their knowledge of Catholicism. The IFG also provides discernment for ongoing formation and enables the sessions at the Institute Day to address apparent weaknesses and to point out areas that need to be improved.

The diocese in conjunction with St. Francis University also conducts a two week program for teachers during the early part of June that provides catechetical content and methodology. Approximately 300 teachers have taken these courses which focus on the four pillars of the *Catechism of the Catholic*

Church. The teachers value learning the content in these important areas, while growing in what they describe as an "adult faith" and gaining new confidence for teaching.

Finally, for 20 years the diocese has received a continual flow of grant funds from Our Sunday Visitor for Theological formation. Sixty-five people have received an MA in Theology and 20 are presently perusing this goal, which has provided a tremendous gift of expertise for various levels of formation.

In summary, the factors that have enhanced strong faith formation in the diocese are:

- A bishop who is personally involved and constantly motivational for principals, teachers and students.

- The conformity of the formation with significant documents of the Church; namely *Catechesis Tradendae*, the *Catechism of the Catholic Church*, the *General Directory of Catechesis* of 1997, and the *National Directory of Catechesis* of 2005.

- The ongoing funding for 20 years from Our Sunday Visitor totaling over $1.4 million.

- The consistency of the yearly Institute Days over 20 years.

- Having the Diocesan Director in place for 22 years. There have been four Catholic School Superintendents during this time but formation programs have been sustained.

- The screening and selection process of those who pursue the MA in Theology surfacing talented catechists.

- The availability of so many teachers with Master's degrees in Theology. They provide leadership and constitute the majority of those who continue to teach in various programs of adult formation throughout the diocese.

- The strong spirit of respect and collaboration between the Catholic Schools Office and the Office of Catechesis.

- The collegial spirit that exists between the diocese and the universities of Notre Dame and St. Francis.

- The positive attitudes of the teachers, knowing that their efforts in the schools are bearing fruit.

- The growing trend of having full-time religion teachers for grades 6, 7 and 8.

Sister M. Jane Carew, OV
Director of Religious Education
Diocese of Fort Wayne-South Bend

ACRE: A Success Story for The Diocese of St. Petersburg

ACRE has been utilized as a part of the religious education assessment process for Catholic schools and parish religious education programs in the Diocese of St. Petersburg since 1995. A policy for the use of ACRE on an annual basis in grades five, eight and eleven was promulgated in 1994 and ACRE was used for the first time in the spring of 1995. ACRE's first generation assessment tool (1992 edition) established an awareness of the need to assess in some objective ways, both the efficacy of religious education instruction (parish and Catholic school) as well as the affective sense of Church relatedness/connectedness of those enrolled in school and parish programs. The second edition of ACRE (2001 Edition) was used for the first time in 2002 during the spring assessment time frame. For the Diocese of St. Petersburg, the assessment is scheduled by the parish and school programs at any time during the March 1 through April 30 time frame and according to local calendar preferences.

Overall, the use of the ACRE has had positive results in affirming the strengths of programs and establishing strategies to address areas of program weakness or need. Over the years, innovations in instructional methods and implementation of new curricula were either affirmed or challenged as I will discuss later in this report.

A word about the implementation of ACRE as recommended in the manuals is needed before addressing the expected as well as unexpected but also positive outcomes for the religious education programs in our diocese. In my experience, it has been repeatedly demonstrated that the ACRE process has been most effective when parish and school leaders and teachers/catechists have carefully implemented the curriculum alignment as laid out in Appendices A—C in the *Administration and Interpretation Manual*. Where the investment of time has been given to predicting student responses and reviewing and comparing the group reports at the conclusion of the assessment to those predictions, there is ample evidence of program growth and development over the years. Where the alignment process has not been undertaken, there has been less evidence of the application of new strategies for instruction and less growth in structured in-service and formation for catechists.

Where the ACRE alignment process has been implemented, parish and Catholic school pastors and catechetical/educational leaders have reported a high level of satisfaction with ACRE. Likewise, they have indicated a positive influence on their selection and use of curriculum materials as well as their development of teacher/catechist in-service plans designed to enhance teaching of content that is weakest in terms of incorrect student responses. Faith formation leaders have been using the program weaknesses outlined in the group reports as the basis for their selection and purchase of the religious education materials that are strongest in those areas of demonstrated student need. These leaders report they are more confident that better instructional coverage of those topics will be provided in the future. This is also true of their selection and purchase of supplemental teaching materials (audio-visuals, home activities, online resources and the like).

From my perspective, there is clear evidence that in these situations, the entire parish/school community has a better awareness of both the value and effectiveness of the catechetical programs in which their children are enrolled. I also attribute the clear data that ACRE provides as the reason why these parish faith formation programs and Catholic Schools tend to provide more feedback and input to the parents of their students, thus maximizing the partnership of parish/school with parents in the education and formation of children. In Catholic school programs in particular, the ACRE data are shared with the entire school community along with other academic progress reports. These outcomes alone have made the use of ACRE a success story for the Diocese of St. Petersburg.

Most helpful have been some unanticipated (when ACRE became policy and practice) but extremely positive developments in catechetical programs over time. These include:

1. A realization that the content areas for which the catechists lacked firm and up-to-date understandings (as determined by the use of *Information for Growth*, the adult formation inventory tool, another product of The Department of Religious Education of the National Catholic Educational Association) were consistent with those same domains and content areas

for which students demonstrated a similar lack of clear understanding on the ACRE assessment. For example, comparison of the results on both the ACRE and IFG showed similar patterns of incorrect responses to questions about conscience-based decision making, knowledge of church history, and "Vatican II" terms and expressions such as "people of God" and "preferential option for the poor." These correlations led to the development of new segments of the Diocesan Catechist Certification Program for adult learners and revamped curriculum guidelines for student programs that better emphasized objectives related to *Life in Christ, Church History* and *Catholic Faith Literacy*—all of these, domains of ACRE. In this way, ACRE figured greatly in the improvement of both content emphasis and catechist formation with both students and catechists demonstrating improved response levels, and most importantly, better faith knowledge.

2. As parishes have looked to new instructional innovations in faith formation programs, there has been, as usually exists with any change, concern that new methods of catechizing do not result in a decline in faith knowledge acquisition. While there has been interest in improving relational catechesis efforts, no one would want to do so at the expense of content learning. The happy result has been solid evidence that not only has content learning been maintained, but it has improved and, **equally important**, there is great improvement in the desirable responses in the affective assessment portion of ACRE in those programs adopting newer instructional strategies. One parish that began a two week, all day summer session with quarterly annual lectionary driven catechetical gatherings reported not only higher *Faith Knowledge* student scores than those of the "regular weekly session students" but also more positive *Affective* responses. This has been especially true in areas reflecting on the students' sense of connectedness and rapport with the parish community and their catechists. Not surprisingly, there is evidence, though as yet not empirically measured (but nonetheless observed by the Catechetical Leader), that weekly, yearlong Mass attendance is at an improved rate for the "summer program" students. This once experimental effort is now solidly part of the parish's program.

3. ACRE has provided our Catholic schools with an opportunity to celebrate the effectiveness of their faith formation programs and their development of the Catholic identity of their students. Since 2006, the annual report of the Catholic Schools of the Diocese of St. Petersburg has featured the diocesan Catholic schools profile of ACRE scores vis-à-vis national norms. This has become a point of pride for our Bishop, the Pastors, and the Administrators and Faculty of the Catholic schools. For many years information about the secular curricular, extra and co-curricular strengths of the Catholic schools were touted. Standardized testing scores, college entrance statistics and other outstanding achievements were highlighted. In an effort to affirm the essential mission of Catholic schools, the addition of the ACRE scores has not only bolstered the image of our schools, it has provided renewed impetus for making Catholic schools understood as more clearly aligned to the evangelizing and catechizing mission of the Church. Schools are affirmed for their excellence in religious education and in turn faith knowledge and affective rapport of students with the Church is showing continued growth—proof that "nothing succeeds like success!"

These three particular success stories about ACRE give testimony to the efficacy of assessment that is intended not so much as a simple measure of learning, but more so as the seeds of continued growth and enhancement of formation programs and learning for children, youth and adults.

Brian A. Lemoi
Director: Office of Evangelization & Lifelong Faith Formation
Diocese of St. Petersburg

ACRE in the Diocese of Arlington

The Religion Program

The religion curriculum for the Catholic schools of the Diocese of Arlington was developed in conjunction with the Diocesan Office of Catechist Formation. The curriculum is intended to assist catechists in fulfilling the mission of the Church to educate children in the fullness of the Catholic Faith: (a) to believe what the Creed teaches; (b) to participate in the liturgical and sacramental life of the Church; (c) to live a life of love for God and neighbor; and (d) to pray to the Father through Jesus, His Son, in the Spirit.

The framework of the religion curriculum for grades PK – 8 is designed and structured around a center: the mystery of the Blessed Trinity and of Christ, as expressed in the four Pillars of the *Catechism of the Catholic Church:*

1. The Profession of Faith – Creed

2. The Celebration of the Christian Mystery – Sacraments

3. Life in Christ – Commandments and the Moral Life

4. Christian Prayer – Prayer

Emphasis on "terms and prayers to know" and targeted virtues at each grade level are added dimensions to the four Pillars. This particular configuration within the religion curriculum works well for our teachers and students.

The identified goals for each grade as well as preparation for the Sacrament of Confirmation are as follows:

- PRE-K AND KINDERGARTEN: To develop the Roman Catholic Identity of the child—individually, within the family and within the parish.

- GRADE 1: To provide a general introduction to the Catholic Faith. The student will be helped to come to knowledge of God: Father, Son and Holy Spirit.

- GRADE 2: To help the student begin to understand the sacramental life of the Church, especially the Sacraments of Penance and the Eucharist.

147

- GRADE 3: To help the student come to a deeper understanding of the Church as a community of faith to which he/she belongs by virtue of Baptism.

- GRADE 4: To have the student understand that followers of Jesus Christ are called to witness to the Good News of Salvation to others and to help build up the Kingdom of God as we journey to our heavenly goal.

- GRADE 5: To have the student come to a more thorough understanding of the Sacraments, the Liturgy, and the Creed.

- GRADE 6: To have the student understand that God's saving actions and His love are manifested in salvation history and fulfilled in Jesus.

- GRADE 7: To have the student understand that God's saving action in salvation history culminates in the person and ministry of Jesus Christ and in the eternal life He offers us.

- GRADE 8: To have the student understand the meaning of the Church, its mission in the world, and their responsibility to participate in that mission.

- CONFIRMATION: To have the students realize the added strength received in Confirmation as their baptismal promises are sealed in receiving the gift of the Holy Spirit, which binds them more closely to the Church and deepens their commitment to be a witness for Jesus to spread and defend the Faith.

The curriculum for the high school students is currently in the revision process to comply with the Religion Framework of the United States Conference of Catholic Bishops (USCCB). The freshman courses have been developed for implementation for the current school year. The remaining courses are in the process of being developed.

Certification

In order to teach the religion program effectively, the Diocese of Arlington has instituted a program of catechist certification, which all religion teachers are required to obtain. The requirements for this certification are spelled out in the document "Go Therefore." This program requires the teachers to obtain certification by their third year teaching in the diocese. There are two levels of certification: Basic and Advanced.

To obtain Basic certification a teacher must accumulate 50 points (1 point equals 1 clock hour) comprised of 10 points from the required course, Cat 101 - Catholic Education: What Every Teacher Must Know, and 40 points from either additional courses or other approved sources. Cat 101 is available from the Catholic Education Center online or from the Catholic Distance University. Some examples of other approved sources are: workshops, seminars, retreats, parish lecture series, and spiritual book discussion groups.

Basic certification is valid for five years and may be renewed for another five years by continued education and 10 additional points or upgraded to Advanced by accumulating 50 additional points from courses or other approved sources. Advanced certification is valid for five years and may be renewed for another five years by continued education and 10 additional points.

Student Success

Student success on ACRE can be attributed to a strong curriculum and well-prepared teachers in the Diocese of Arlington. Selecting quality Catholic teachers is a priority with the Diocese. Teacher commitment to imparting and sharing the faith, strong administrative support and parental interest are contributing factors that lead to students not only performing successfully on ACRE, but also in living the Gospel message. The monitoring of curriculum is an essential element of our expectations for quality programs within the schools in the Diocese of Arlington, which is embraced by teachers and administrators.

During 2005-2006, the Office of Catholic Schools reviewed ACRE to determine the level of alignment with the Diocesan religion curriculum. Based on the review, additional assessment items were developed to complement ACRE1 and ACRE2. The review of ACRE3 revealed that the Diocese needed to develop a customized assessment to be more in line with the existing curriculum at that time, as well as now, in light of the USCCB framework. As the high school frameworks are being developed for the various courses, appropriately aligned assessments will be developed.

Components of Arlington's Success

The unique and especially effective components of the religion program of the Diocese of Arlington are:

• Enthusiastic and committed teachers;

• Catechist certification requirements;

• Well-developed curriculum;

• Effective use of the diocesan monitoring sheets to ensure that all elements of the curriculum are covered;

• Priestly presence in the religion classroom;

• Multi-text approach to the teaching of religion;

• Use of textbooks approved by the Office of Catholic Schools.

To this list, we would add the support of the parents. Our schools strive to develop a strong relationship, helping parents to understand and support our religion program. The combination of school and home, when possible, is the ideal.

Monitoring the Religion Program

The results from ACRE are analyzed and discussed at the local level, as well as on the Diocesan level. The review of the test results provides insights as to the elements within the curriculum that need to be reinforced and/or supported in order to provide a strong foundation for the faith development of the students. Individual meetings related to the assessments are conducted annually with each principal and administration at the Office of Catholic Schools. The results from ACRE are among the various assessments that are reviewed and discussed in light of advancing student performance and programs.

Conclusion

Aware that programs can always be improved and must be constantly moni-totored, the Office of Catholic Schools continues to pay close attention to the religion program in the schools. Summer workshops, sessions at diocesan professional development days, discussions at principals' meetings and assessment as part of the school accreditation process are all ways to keep this topic in the forefront of our consciousness. Only in this way can we continue to fulfill our mission as Catholic Schools.

Lastly, we believe that we must cultivate the home and school relationship, using the school program to reach families and strengthen their Christian life. Then truly we are Catholic schools.

Sister Bernadette McManigal, BVM
Superintendent of Schools
Diocese of Arlington, Virginia

ACRE and Religious Education
in the Diocese of Houma-Thibodaux

The goal of catechesis/religious education is to foster a relationship with Jesus Christ that leads to maturity in faith. Such maturity will only be achieved through a lifelong pursuit of prayerful faith formation based on the realization that "the love of God has been poured out in our hearts through the Holy Spirit who has been given to us." (Romans 5:5) In the formative years knowing where one stands in relation to knowledge of faith and faith awareness can help engender a desire to know more about God and the Church.

As educators in Catholic schools how can we evaluate if our goal has been achieved? Such an evaluation calls for a thorough review of the religion curriculum, teaching methods, instructional approaches and available resources allocated to accomplish the mission. It is true that no single evaluative paper and pencil instrument can measure a person's love of God or faith. By integrating "head" knowledge with desires of the heart, that is, personal beliefs, attitudes, practices, and perceptions, ACRE offers a profile of faith formation that is well integrated.

Research indicates that ACRE is a valid and reliable evaluation tool for religion programs. Desiring to evaluate the outcomes of our Catholic school religion programs in the Diocese of Houma-Thibodaux, I encouraged fifth, eighth and tenth grades in all of my schools to administer the ACRE assessment. ACRE assesses the basic faith knowledge and religious perceptions of students at various age levels and stages of development. With the results teachers are able to identify areas of strength as well as areas that need improvement and to adjust the curriculum and teaching strategies to address these findings. After each grade is tested, teachers determine what concepts students did not master and focus on those areas in the preceding and following grade levels. Principals and religion coordinators have been successful in monitoring student progress and evaluating their religion program by studying their ACRE results. As the superintendent, reviewing the ACRE assessment results annually allows me to identify the trajectory of our faith education efforts and track improvements as goals and strategies are changed and refined.

A strong religious formation program provides students with solid instruction based on the knowledge and love of Jesus Christ and his teaching, coupled with an experience of a nurturing faith community that inspires a discipleship of service. Stability and continuity of curriculum is of utmost importance in the religion curriculum. For over twenty years all of the elementary schools in the Diocese of Houma-Thibodaux have used the William Sadlier religion textbooks series as the basis for our religion education curriculum. The Sadlier religion series contains the basic concepts of our Catholic faith. Over the years we have determined that the mastery of the Sadlier series skills prepares our students for the areas assessed on ACRE. Professional in-services are always provided to our teachers when revised religion editions are introduced. This is a key to the success of any religion program.

Teachers who educate in the faith must be attuned to the mission, goals, and strategies inherent to the delivery of sound catechesis; therefore, all teachers of religion are required to have diocesan basic certification before being allowed to teach Catholic school religion. The following is a description of the Houma-Thibodaux Diocesan certification program:

Bayou Foundations Course
Catholic Adult Faith Formation Program

The Bayou Foundations Course is an adult education process, dynamic and participatory which reflects our Catholic tradition, individual experience and input, critical reflection and group formation. This comprehensive program for catechists, teachers, youth ministers, Confirmation staff, Small Christian Community participants, and Evangelization team members provides a foundation for Adult Faith Formation to deepen faith, develop a vision and skills for ministry, and enhance theological understanding. The design is group oriented led by qualified presenters knowledgeable and experienced in pastoral ministry and adult learning theory.

Introduction to Theology Objectives:

• Become familiar with the Vatican II paradigm shift in understanding revelation: What it is, how it happens and what is revealed?

• Be aware of how revelation is handed on and developed in the church

• Be alerted to how we participate in this process

• Distinguish between faith, theology and doctrine and understand how they need to be connected in the life of the church.

Human Development & Communication

Session 1: Reflective Listening

Session 2: James Fowler's Stages of Faith Development

Session 3: Cultural Assumption

Session 4: Conflict, Consensus, Cultural Analysis

Session 5: Consensus, Cultural Analysis, Cultural Diversity

Hebrew Scriptures

Session 1: Introduction to People, Land and Text of Hebrew Scriptures

Session 2: Exodus and Covenant

Session 3: Genesis 1 -11 Ancestors of Jews and United Kingdom

Session 4: United Kingdom Divided; The 8th Century Prophets

Session 5: Exile, Prophets, Restoration

Session 6: Prayer, Wisdom, and Apocalyptic Literature

Christian Scriptures

Session 1: Introduction/Ministry of Jesus/Paul

Session 2: Paul: Galatians, Romans and 1 Corinthians

Session 3: Paul and Introduction to Mark

Session 4: Mark, Matthew and Luke

Session 5: Matthew, Luke and John

Session 6: John and Summary

Church

Session 1: Jesus' Culture and Times, Early Church Development

Session 2: Church Structure, Theology and Worship 2nd & 3rd Centuries

Session 3: Liturgy/Sacraments in the 4th and 5th Centuries

Session 4: Early Church Vision and Reforms of Vatican II

Session 5: Vatican II Church

Session 6: World Church

Sacraments and Prayer

Session 1: Understanding Prayer and Symbols

Session 2: Sacramentality, Liturgy - Ritual

Session 3: Sacraments of Initiation

Session 4: Major Themes of Eucharistic Theology

Session 5: Current Eucharistic language, practice and theology

Session 6: Personal Prayer

In addition to diocesan religious education certification, all Catholic school personnel are required to participate in faculty and school prayer, liturgy, attend an annual faculty retreat and be a personal witness to one another and the students to whom they serve.

The vision of the Catholic School Office has always been to form students who know the mind and heart of Jesus Christ and to be viable witnesses in the world of tomorrow. Through the dedication of our conscientious faculties, students are encouraged to not only know their faith but to live it through discipleship. This coupled with our stable religion curriculum continues to make our program exceptional, as evidenced by our students' high performance on ACRE.

Sister Immaculata Paisant M.S.C.
Superintendent of Catholic Schools
Diocese of Houma-Thibodaux

Religious Education at St. Julie Billiart Parish
Hamilton, Ohio

Brief History of St. Julie Billiart Parish

In 1989 three parishes, St. Stephen, St Mary's and St. Veronica's merged to become St. Julie Billiart Parish. St. Julie Billiart is located downtown in the city of Hamilton, Ohio. The parish currently serves around 800 families, with a rich mix of White, non-Hispanic and Hispanic families. Most of our English speaking parishioners fall into a lower middle socio-economic class.

In 1999, St. Julie Billiart became one of three Hispanic centers in the Archdiocese of Cincinnati. Our current pastor is bilingual, which has been a great asset to our Hispanic community. The Hispanic center is manned by a lay missionary from Mexico and a Franciscan priest who works at the center Friday through Sunday. While we still maintain a weekly Sunday liturgy in Spanish, we started to celebrate sacraments bilingually as well as whole parish catechesis programs and the Easter Triduum.

Description of the Religious Education Program

Until recently the two communities ran parallel but separate religious education programs. In September 2008 we combined the programs. In the Hispanic tradition catechesis only takes place immediately before the reception of a sacrament. We identified two areas of concern which prompted our merger. First, the children speak and learn in English. The catechists for the program only spoke Spanish or very little English and the textbooks they were using were in Spanish. Secondly, the catechists lacked any formal training.

We currently have 120 students in the Religious Education Program, 70 are Caucasian, non-Hispanic and 50 are Hispanic. We closed our parochial school in 2008 and formed a collaborative school with another parish, St. Peter in Chains. Sixty-one children from the parish attend the collaborative. The Parish Religious Education program is also responsible for the sacramental preparation of those students. We have a few families that attend other Catholic schools and some that are home schooled as well.

We offer faith formation classes from first grade through high school. We also offer three additional sacramental classes. We have 15 children preparing for Baptism and First Eucharist, a class of eight older students preparing for First Communion, and a class of six students preparing for Baptism on the feast of Pentecost.

Confirmation is celebrated in our parish every other year for seventh and eighth graders. Last year we had 83 Confirmandi and celebrated a bilingual Mass. We are offering Confirmation again this year for 26 candidates to get on the same schedule as our collaborative school.

Catechist Recruitment and Training

Like most parishes we recruit catechists on the basis of personal invitation and lots of prayers. In more than 30 years in faith formation I have never experienced a waiting line of people dying to become catechists. One method that I use and that has been quite helpful is that the staff takes turns meeting and interviewing new parishioners. This year I was able to recruit two catechists who had served in their prior parishes and also had some catechetical classes under their belt.

The Hispanic ministry also gave me the name of one of their catechists who is a teacher and is bilingual. She teaches the older class of First Communicants and is a blessing, as she provides a sense of belonging and familiarity to our Hispanic students.

I also have volunteer mothers assisting the catechists in a variety of needs. As they get familiar with the program over the years and their interest increases, I have been able to encourage several of them to move to the next level and try their hand as a catechist.

The Archdiocese of Cincinnati has a program for educating catechists. Our catechists are encouraged to take these classes, which the parish pays for. This year we also offered a stipend to the catechists that helps them cover gas and babysitting fees. As these classes are offered at various locations throughout the archdiocese, travel can be an issue for the catechists, so I offer at least one class a year on campus.

Staff meetings also provide another venue for training as well as for individual conferences. If an individual catechist is struggling, I find that sometimes role modeling a couple of classes for the catechist can be effective. Finally, providing catechists with new ideas and techniques for their classes has produced great growth.

What Makes Our Program Special

Our program spends a great deal of effort in planning rituals and events that help to make faith come alive. We try to involve the parents and the whole faith community in our activities. Our parish has a monthly newsletter, *St. Julie's Jewels.* This is a wonderful vehicle to promote and report on the various activities in our program. The role of our pastor is key; he supports the program and is actively involved in it. The students see him in the classroom not just the church.

The following are a few examples or highlights of our program:

Young Vincentians

Young Vincentians is an outreach group that provides our students a means of putting their faith into action. They have made lunches for a homeless shelter, conducted bake sales, and participated in the "Share Your Christmas Blessings" clothing and used toy drive for the women's homeless shelter. They are also scheduled to hold "Game nights" at a local nursing home.

Family Days

Parents are invited to come to classes and share in our learning activities. This fall's theme was St. Paul. The junior high students prepared a skit on the life of St. Paul and then later the parents and students made scripture door signs for our parish shut-ins and local nursing home. Parents were asked to bring in individual wrapped snacks which we put stickers on saying that we were praying for our policemen and firemen and thanking them for their service. We had parents distribute boxes of snacks to the stations. At Christmas our Hispanic parents did a Posada for the children.

Whole Parish Catechesis

Thus far we have had two major events. The first was "Honoring Mary around the World" for which we adapted Sadlier's prepared program. Parishioners were invited to bring in their favorite ethnic dish to share as we studied Marian shrines. They were also asked to bring in their Marian sacramentals, which we displayed in the church for two Sundays.

The other event was for the feast of Corpus Christi. Parishioners were asked to bring in their First Communion pictures and date them. The pictures were displayed in the church by the decades in which they were taken. We had pictures dating from 1899 through the present. After Mass we had a procession around our church neighborhood with the Eucharist. The events are done bilingually.

Special Additions to our Programs

Our Rite of Enrollment is held on the Feast celebrating the Baptism of the Lord. First Communicants are asked to bring their Baptismal candle to Mass and they are lit from the Paschal candle during the rite. This year one of our First Communicants had a new sister being baptized during this Mass and our pastor combined the two rites. The children were able to gather around the Baptismal font and watch the baptism.

Each of our First Communicants has a member of the community who prays for them during the course of the year. We give each prayer partner a picture of their First Communicant in September. They are then invited to come at the end of our First Communion retreat day and meet the child and their parents. We take pictures of the prayer partner and First Communicant together and give them to them later as a parish gift.

Confirmation preparation includes three prayer services for parents, sponsors, and candidates. The themes are on each of the three sacraments of initiation.

We bring in guest speakers to talk about different timely topics to all the classes. For example, we had a member of the Sisters of Notre Dame come and share with us about Dorothy Stang, a member of their community and a native Ohioan who was martyred in Brazil. Kris Kringle appeared in December. We have had a professional children's group come and perform Christian music.

Two new features we are adding this year are teaching prayers in both English and Spanish, and adding a liturgical music class.

Use of the ACRE test

I usually write a report for the pastor on our results from ACRE. This gives me an opportunity to study the results, spot the domains where we have strengths and weaknesses, and look at the particular questions that seem to be giving our students difficulties. Sometimes it is as simple as determining that the language in the ACRE is different from what my catechists are using. A case in point is "The Lord's Prayer" vs. "Our Father." At a catechist meeting we go over first our strengths so that the catechist can feel positive about their instruction and then discuss areas where the children might be struggling. For example, we might discuss how we are teaching about the Trinity. We share ideas and I always try to have new materials available for the catechists regarding the area of concern. We discuss that, even though the children are only tested in the 5th and 8th grades, how well each of those domains are represented in the curriculum of every grade and how we build off of each year's instruction. The ACRE gives us a great tool in planning and identifying areas of our catechetical program where we are succeeding and areas which need our attention.

Alison J. Smith
Coordinator of Religious Education
St. Julie Billiart Parish, Hamilton, Ohio

The Faith Community of St. John the Evangelist School
Hapeville, Georgia

In a Catholic school, a good religion program begins with a well-articulated mission that is embraced by the entire school community. The Mission Statement of St. John the Evangelist School guides policy, establishes the need for programs, and sets the vision.

Our mission is to prepare students for everlasting life by teaching them the Catholic Faith and traditions, to provide time and resources to put their faith into action through worship and service, and to ensure a thorough foundation of knowledge for successful transition into secondary study.

If we are to transform hearts and souls, religious formation must go beyond formal instruction. The effective components of the religious program at St. John the Evangelist School include morning assembly, vibrant worship, the daily presence of clergy, relevant service and cultural inclusion.

The gathering together as a school family each morning fosters a strong faith community and links the rich spiritual traditions of our Catholic faith to the present generation of students. Morning assembly affords many opportunities to enrich our religion program in areas assessed by ACRE (Church History, Prayer/ Religious Practices, Scripture, Liturgy and Sacraments). At morning assembly, the principal sets a spiritual tone for the day and introduces traditional prayers, such as the Spiritual Rosary. Faculty members also introduce prayers and share "faith stories" that connect these prayers to their hearts. A Christmas Novena, the Divine Chaplet, the Memorare and the Angelus are prayers that have special meaning to the faculty. Prayer requests are received daily because people in the school community know from experience the power of prayer. For serious or grave intentions, prayers are offered on the hour. Praying for others by name and as a whole faith community is a powerful experience which binds us as a school family.

During morning assembly, students and faculty prepare for vibrant worship on Friday. Significant faith concepts (Paschal Mystery, Trinity), feast days (Ascension/Assumption, Pentecost), seasons of the church or lives of the saints are discussed, and common misconceptions identified in ACRE are clarified. Before adoration of the Blessed Sacrament, the monstrance is displayed and the rays extending from the monstrance are compared to the grace that flows into us when we come before Jesus in adoration. Age-appropriate guided meditations deepen the adoration experience. Students are reminded that sharing Eucharist with one another is the most important thing we do all week.

At a time when Catholic schools hunger for a visible presence of clergy, we are fortunate to have a deacon present every day. He serves as athletic director, substitute teacher, homilist at Friday masses and service coordinator. He brings a spiritual dimension to the classrooms, the athletic field, sermons at Friday liturgies and service projects. He is often joined on the altar by other deacons who are grandparents of students at the school. These dedicated men model the call to religious vocations for the students.

Relevant community service reinforces Life in Christ and Catholic Social Teaching assessed by ACRE. Speakers share personal experiences and describe the needs of those whom they serve: Soldiers returning from Iraq (Card Project), Youth Shelter Director (School Supplies Project); CDC Director (Nothin' but Nets Project - mosquito nets that save lives of children in Africa), and Hospice Nurse (Cancer Home Project), are but a few examples. At Mass a special "service cross" is blessed and passed to the class directing the current whole school service project. The cross serves as a visual reminder of the work we do in Jesus' name.

Cultural inclusion is displayed by a framed cross with photographs of the faces of every student, faculty and staff member. In the center of the cross is the face of Jesus who unites us as one school family. School events include cultural customs such as Las Posadas, the Heritage Museum, International Night, liturgical dances and Thanksgiving customs from around the world. Students in native dress present a visual representation of the world around us, yet as we gather around the table of the Lord, we are brothers and sisters in Christ. Visiting priests representing our many cultures speak of the customs of their native lands and share how they received God's call to the priesthood.

Respect for and knowledge of other faith traditions is encouraged and practiced. Diversity studies and religion classes take a look at other world religions with the goal of producing young people who are strong in their faith yet tolerant and informed about others.

Teachers play a major role in faith formation through the faith experiences and knowledge they bring to the classroom. The ACRE and the IFG assessment provide objective views of faculty strengths and areas for further development. Based on results, professional development targets areas of need. These may include catechetical training, retreat experiences, and formal instruction in methodology. Sound instructional resources, opportunities for teachers to collaborate, share best practices and mentor one another enhance our faith programs and benefit both teachers and students.

Another effective evaluative measure of our programs is the Curriculum Alignment Review, Appendix C, in the ACRE interpretation manual. This exercise helps teachers become familiar with topics in ACRE and helps identify when, where and how the topics are addressed. Super Standards are identified ("I won't leave 4th grade without knowing....") and appropriate expectations are set at each grade level. Teachers chart curriculum standards/benchmarks addressed each quarter and a curriculum map is generated from completed lesson plans.

The administrative team analyzes ACRE results beyond the national scores. This provides valuable insight into performance standards and is an objective means of measuring students' attitudes, beliefs and practices. Further analysis helps to answer questions such as: Are lower scores made by new students, returning students, or non-Catholic students? Close examination of students' answers pinpoints misconceptions and prompts discussion of an effective plan of action to address the needs of the community. Students' actions toward others on and off campus, informal conversations with fellow students and teachers, and journal reflections and essays further indicate the extent that faith has taken root in their hearts.

The religion program at St. John the Evangelist School, with the mission as its foundation, combines daily formal instruction and an active prayer life.

Our school motto, "Reverence, Respect and Responsibility," and themes such as, "Servants, Scholars and Saints" and "Grace, Gratitude and Giving" foster core Catholic values that are applied to all aspects of school life. Relevant service opportunities bind the community together as we see Christ in every face we encounter. We cherish these values, nurture them, and present them continuously by example in our daily lives. With diligent attention to the religion program, both in its formal and informal aspects, we prepare the next generation of Catholics to know, love and serve the Lord in an ever changing world.

Karen Vogtner
Principal
St. John the Evangelist School [1], Hapeville, Georgia

---

[1] St. John the Evangelist School is a U. S. Department of Education Blue Ribbon School of Excellence located in the Archdiocese of Atlanta. The School enrolls 287 students in grades PK-8. Ninety-two percent of the students are Catholic, with almost three-quarters from racial/ethnic minority populations: 45 percent African American, 15 percent Asian, and 13 percent Hispanic. NCEA has recognized Karen Vogtner as a Distinguished Elementary School Principal.

References

Carroll, J. B. (1963). A model of school learning. *Teachers College Record,* 64, 723-733.

Cohen, J. (1988). *Statistical power analysis for the behavioral sciences* (2nd Ed.). Hillsdale, NJ: Lawrence Erlbaum and Associates.

Coleman, J. S. (1988). Social capital in the creation of human capital. *American Journal of Sociology, 94, Supplement,* S95-S120.

Congregation for Catholic Education (September 8, 2009). Religious education in schools fits into the evangelizing mission of the Church. Vatican City.

Convey, J. J. (1992). *Catholic schools make a difference: Twenty-five years of research.* Washington, DC: National Catholic Educational Association.

Convey, J. J., & Thompson, A. D. (1999). *Weaving Christ's seamless garment: Assessment of Catholic religious education.* Washington, DC: National Catholic Educational Association.

National Catholic Educational Association (2002). *NCEA ACRE interpretation manual.* Washington, DC: National Catholic Educational Association

Nunnally, J. C. (1978). *Psychometric theory* (2nd Ed.). New York: McGraw-Hill.

Smith, C. (2005). *Soul searching.* New York: Oxford University Press.

Thompson, A. D. (1982). *That they may know you . . .* Washington, DC: National Catholic Educational Association.

United States Catholic Conference (1994). *Catechism of the Catholic Church.* Washington, DC: United States Catholic Conference.

United States Catholic Conference (1997). *Protocol for assessing the conformity of catechetical materials with the Catechism of the Catholic Church.* Washington, DC: United States Catholic Conference.

About the Author

John J. Convey is the St. Elizabeth Ann Seton Professor of Education and former Provost at The Catholic University of America. Dr. Convey joined the faculty at CUA in 1974 and served as Provost from 1997 to 2007.

Dr. Convey received his Ph.D. in research and evaluation from The Florida State University in 1974, a M.S. in mathematics from The Ohio State University in 1968 and a B.A. in mathematics from La Salle College in 1962. During the 1986–87 academic year, he was a Senior Research Fellow in the Office of Research at the United States Department of Education.

His professional work focuses on research and strategic planning for Catholic schools. Over the past 28 years, he has conducted diocesan-wide planning and evaluation studies for the Catholic schools in the Archdioceses of Atlanta, Baltimore, Boston, Denver and Washington and the Dioceses of Alexandria (Louisiana), Biloxi, Brooklyn, Charlotte, Cheyenne, Corpus Christi, Honolulu, and Providence. He is currently conducting planning studies for the Archdiocese of Mobile.

Dr. Convey is the author or editor of seven books on Catholic education: *Catholic Schools Make A Difference: Twenty-five Years of Research* (1992), *Strategic Planning for Catholic Schools: A Diocesan Model of Consultation* (1996), *Benchmarks of Excellence: Diocesan and Local Catholic School Boards* (1997), *Weaving Christ's Seamless Garment: Assessment of Catholic Religious Education* (1999), *Catholic Schools at the Crossroads: Survival and Transformation* (2000), *The Catholic Character of Catholic Schools* (2000), and *Weathering the Storm: Moving Catholic Schools Forward* (2009), as well as many articles.

Dr. Convey was the 1991 recipient of the C. Albert Koob Award, given by the National Catholic Educational Association for outstanding national service to Catholic schools. In November 2005 he was awarded the *Benemerenti Medal* by Pope Benedict XVI in recognition of his service to The Catholic University of America and to Catholic schools. He is a Commissioner on the Middle States Commission on Higher Education and a consultant to the Committee on Catholic Education of the United States Conference of Catholic Bishops.